Ivan Mauger's Speedway Spectacular

Edited by

IVAN MAUGER AND PETER OAKES

PELHAM BOOKS

First published in Great Britain by
PELHAM BOOKS LTD
52 Bedford Square
London, W.C.1.
1975

ISBN 0 7207 0725 0

Set and printed in Great Britain
by Hollen Street Press Ltd at Slough
and bound by Dorstel Press at Harlow, Essex

Contents

Acknowledgements

The authors' thanks are due to the following who have helped in the compilation of this book: Lars Edgren, Peter White, Ian MacDonald, Jeff Collerton, Michael Patrick, Ivan Crozier, Ian Hoskins, Philip Rising, Andrew Edwards, Peter Strong, Paul Parish, Dave Booth, Dave Stevens and Gay Robbins.

Also to the following for their photographs reproduced as illustrations: Ray Page, Klaus Schmidt, Ulrich Ernst, J. Rehounek, Wright Wood, Lars Edgren Pressbild, Michael Patrick, Bruce Kent, Bill Meyer, Rita Mauger, Alf Weedon, Motor Sport-Bilderdrenst, Daily Mirror, Helga Keilwerth, Owen Hines, J. Sergeant, foto-fella, REVS Motor Cycle News.

Foreword

Speedway continues to increase in popularity both in Britain and on the international scene.

One of the men at the centre of this continued expansion is Ivan Mauger—the world famous triple crown winner.

A spectacular sport and a spectacular personality—what better title could we have for this book than: SPECTACULAR.

Within the covers is presented an international study of the present state of Speedway in what may come to be regarded as its Golden Age.

Top international journalists—men such as Peter White, Ian MacDonald and Dave Booth—have teamed up with some of the top men in the sport; riders, managers and promoters; to explain the sport worldwide in this authoritative but entertaining book.

Top photographers—men like Mike Patrick—have produced action photographs of the stars at work and play.

Whatever your interests in Speedway this book has something for you.

A moment of decision . . .

1
MY SPEEDWAY FUTURE
by Ivan Mauger

I have been riding speedway since I was at school—and that takes me back eighteen years. Soon I will have been in the sport for two decades. And it is this lifetime in the game that prompts people to ask me: When are you going to retire?

Naturally it is a subject that I have thought about in recent times and once or twice I have been on the knife-edge verge of quitting the sport. In fact before I joined my current club, Exeter, on a three-year contract, I was within an hour of hanging up my leathers for good.

Many things about speedway at that time had sickened me and I called a press conference—originally to announce my retirement from speedway.

But at the last minute Exeter came forward with a contract that I would have been a fool not to sign. It would help ensure my future security once I have finished as a rider . . . and guaranteed me at least three settled years at one track.

That contract ends when the last race of the 1975 season has been run and it would seem an appropriate time to swap my riding leathers for a businessman's suit and concentrate solely on off-track commitments.

For the last couple of years I have been involved in a couple of business ventures and the success of the inaugural World Champions Series—which Barry Briggs and I set up—proved to me that I could probably make more money on that side of the sport than by riding.

I have no doubt that I will be involved in speedway in one way or another for the rest of my days . . . but how long riding?

At one time during the early days of this season I had made up my mind that once my Exeter contract finishes I will finish riding.

Certainly I still feel that I will see out my days in the West Country but I am still not certain whether that will be at the end of the 1975 season . . . or a little later.

Because the one thing that will determine my retirement date is my ability.

Among my characteristics and idiosyncracies I include pride and stubbornness. Pride would not allow me to continue riding if I didn't genuinely think I could be capable of being the world's best—and stubbornness would ensure that once I had made my decision to quit I would stick to it.

I couldn't bear to go out in a meeting and lose races consistently. Fortunately throughout my career I have been able to judge my own ability and I know when I am riding badly. I also know when I have deserved to lose and once I get to the position where I am losing regularly I want no part of riding.

Frankly I don't know when this will be. Maybe it will be tomorrow. Next month. Next year. Or 1980. I am a great believer in physical fitness as being of vital importance in winning and I think it is possible for a rider still to be top of the profession at forty—as long as he is fully fit physically and mentally.

Maybe I will be able to carry on riding until I'm forty but if I am still active I will need to know inwardly that I am still capable—at that age—of winning a World Final.

I would hate to get to the stage where people point at me and say: he used to be World Champion ten years ago.

In my time I have seen too many riders who have carried on riding when they have lost their edge. I don't criticise their decision to keep riding as obviously their mental make-up is far different to mine and they undoubtedly ENJOY riding.

I enjoy it . . . but only because I am winning. I could never claim any enjoyment if I was consistently being beaten by riders I could have given twenty yards start a few seasons earlier.

In the past I have had many disappointments both on a personal—and non-personal—basis and one of those was the lack of response from the sports controlling authorities when I offered to run a national training school for some of the country's bright youngsters.

In recent years riders like John Louis, Peter Collins and Dave Jessup have come through to attain world-class rankings but for every one of them I have seen three others who COULD have made it.

Many is the time I have been to a track and seen a teenager with the skill and ability to provide England with a World Champion. But going back a couple of seasons later they seem to have missed out in some way.

The main reason for this has not been a lack of ability; a lack of skill; a lack of luck; or a lack of courage.

You can put it down to a lack of GUIDANCE.

All too often a youngster has picked up riding faults and had no-one to show him what he is doing wrong. When he is young he can be taught what is the right way and what is the wrong way. As he gets older and more set in his ways it is far more difficult to break the bad habits.

And far too often he develops off-track faults in his general approach and outlook to speedway . . . often encouraged by his closest friends and associates who lap up the publicity that he has attracted and tell him how good he is.

There was a classic example of a young English rider who burst on the scene a few years ago and certainly had all the ingredients to become a possible World Champion.

Several people—myself included—tried to offer him advice and opportunity but he turned it down . . . and decided to try and do it his way.

Today he is still scoring plenty of points for his club—but he has nowhere near realised his full potential and instead of riding in a World Final he is relegated to the role of a Division One heat leader. Had he taken advice offered him in the early stages I am certain he would have qualified for last year's World Final.

Peter Collins shows the other side of the coin. He is quiet and unassuming but when he was a team-mate of mine at Belle Vue he was ever-eager to seek—and take—advice.

As a result he has added an extra dimension to his not inconsiderable natural ability and became England's youngest World Finalist for years.

Similarly John Louis, although a late starter at speedway, listened to what people were telling him—and proved that you don't need to be fresh out of school to make your way to top-flight world-class speedway.

Malcolm Simmons is another classic example of a rider who decided he would listen. For many years Malcolm had a reputation as a rebel-rouser and this overshadowed his actual on-track exploits.

He was a good rider, an international class rider . . . but no more than that.

During the 1972-73 Australian season he sought my advice while I was touring Australia and after I had told him that he needed a more dedicated and professional approach to speedway he became a reformed character.

Since then he has elevated himself into a genuine World Final prospect

Get your wheels in a straight line.

A long-track start.

and won several big open meetings . . . meetings he would have been fortunate to have been selected for twelve months previously.

I think one of the biggest problems facing the young riders today is this lack of encouragement, guidance and advice from authority. Unfortunately there is no-one involved in the sport's administration who has the experience and knowledge of what is needed to become a World Champion.

Many of the people who offer advice never quite made it as a rider and they seem reluctant to call on anyone who has made the final leap from competent performer to world star.

When you consider that Britain has had World Champions like Tommy Price and Freddie Williams it seems a tragedy that they have not been involved in the setting up of a national training school to pass on the finer tips to Britain's best.

In any other sport an ex-champion would have been drafted onto this committee; that committee; and the other committee: but not in speedway.

There are plenty of training schools around doing a most worthwhile job— that is to give young kids the opportunity to ride speedway—but there is a lack of what in schoolgirl parlance would be called a 'finishing school'.

Denmark has already shown the way by sending their top youngsters to spend a week or so with former World Champion Ole Olsen and people like Ole, Barry Briggs and myself are often asked to conduct schools in such places as Italy, Yugoslavia, Finland and Germany.

None of those countries could be termed powerful speedway nations which makes it all the more lamentable that there has been no attempt by Britain to introduce some sort of tuition for the likely prospects . . .

Wedding day . . .

Getting down to it on the long-track.

Travelling in style . . .

Who said the worst traffic jams are in London?

Australian long-tracking at Port Pirie.

Scrambling at Port Noarlunga, South Australia in '66.

Unusual colours—racing at Prague, Czechoslovakia.

The boss and I!

2
SWEDISH SPEEDWAY
by *LARS EDGREN*

This year, no Swedish riders are racing in England. This has caused quite a shock to riders and supporters in Sweden since over the last few years it has been a clear tradition for guest riders from Sweden to be present at the British League.

Swedish riders take, of course, a very dim view of this 'boycott' since the British League has meant such a lot to them. Quite certainly, had it not been for the fact that Swedish stars have been given the opportunity, over a number of years, to ride for British League clubs the standard would not be what it is today in Swedish speedway.

But the intention in this article is to talk about what Swedish speedway has in store below the top few elite riders. Come to think of it, it is rather difficult to give a picture without telling about riders who in one way or another have been in close relationship with British speedway.

Obviously a younger generation is pressing on, challenging for their place among the great also in Sweden.

As a rule, promising riders are transferred from one of the lower divisions (2 and 3) to one of the eight clubs making up the All-Swedish League.

Taking the Eskilstuna Club Smederna, (i.e. The Smiths)—Eskilstuna is the Sheffield of Sweden—who won the First Division in 1973, my view is that they have a most promising rider in Stefan Salomonsson, 24.

Ever since taking up speedway Stefan has had to look after his job as a plumber along with his speedway. This has made it impossible for him to accept, as yet, any British offer. Nevertheless, he has been a member of our Junior National team on quite a few occasions in England and, last autumn, he was entrusted with a place in the Swedish National A-team against Soviet Russia at home at Eskilstuna.

Where Stefan has his strength is in his fighting spirit and his courage.

The Gotland Club, Gotland the island out in the Baltic, Bysarna, won Division I in 1971 and in 1972 relying on a number of club members transferred from other clubs.

Bysarna are however, now concentrating on their own products with a view, possibly, to improve on their performance last year when they won the silver medals.

Sven Nilsson, an engineer, 26, offers the best promise among the riders fostered by the Club itself. Sven took everyone by surprise qualifying for the Swedish Championship Final at Ullevi last year.

Getingarna, 'the Wasps', the Club at the Capital, Stockholm, does not belong to those clubs likely 'to lighten their purse', without thinking it over twice, in order to get hold of good scorers. Their policy has been, over the last few years, to pick out and train some four or five newcomers in their teens for the Club's A-squad. This experiment has proved quite successful and Anders Michanek and Leif Enecrona will be greatly assisted, in this year's racing, by young fellows such as Kent Eriksson, an engineer, 18, Thomas Hydling, a tinsmith, 17, and Richard Hellsén, a motor car engineer, 20. For the present, this trio cannot pride themselves in any performance in the international arena, except Richard who paid a visit, last autumn, to Kings Lynn. But make no mistake, you will hear a lot more about these young riders in the near future.

Stefan Johansson (Dackarna) leads Tommy Jansson (Smederna), Hans Holmkvist (Indianerna) and Hasse Johansson (Ornarna) at Lindesberg in a Swedish Championship meeting.

Anders Michanek   *Christer Lofqvist*

Vargarna, 'the Wolves', from Norrköping, fathered by Arne 'Varg-Far' ('Father-Wolf') Bergström, enjoy a constant reputation for being successful at fostering good youngsters. The veteran, 'Varg-Olle' Nygren is a pure product of the club and, perhaps, the one to have conquered the head-lines more often than the others for the last few years. But Torbjörn Harryson, injured at Wembley in 1969, drove to Vargarna.

Vargarna, too, do not belong to those clubs which are prone to 'extra'— read irregular—handouts to their club mates. It is a pity that over the last few years this attitude should have reduced the number of riders interested in riding for the club.

Anyway, they have a very promising starlet in Thomas Pettersson, a glass-blower, 21. Thomas's record comprises, as his foremost performance, the Swedish Junior Championship for 1972.

For the current year, expectations placed in him were much more far-reaching, perhaps even the securing of a place at the World Championship at Ullevi. Even though he didn't make it he has all that is required in order to achieve just that.

Dackarna, the name taken from the description of gangs of highway robbers in olden times in these remote (in those days) parts of Sweden, at Malilla in Smaland, do have a good deal of their own good riders who for the present are showing their paces mainly on the track at home. Even so Stefan Johansson, 22, a younger brother of the Swedish Champion, Tommy, has a future in store for him as a speedway international. However, quite like Tommy he will never be, but second to him, possibly.

Another Smaland Club in Division I is Njudungarna. This club has, for a series of years, had some difficulty in keeping their position in the top division. Their material has not at all times been up to the mark—a fact which largely is due to their categorical refusal to take in riders from outside clubs. Lars-Ake Anderson is a product of their own with some prospects for the future. However, he is developing rather slowly in spite of having stayed in England at the Olle Nygren Speedway School and in the Junior Team. Perhaps 1974 will be his year, let us wait and see.

Ornarna, (The Eagles) at Mariestad has, in the main, just Bengt Larsson and he is, of course, well-known to English speedway enthusiasts after a succession of years at Sheffield Tigers. It can be said of Börje Klingberg, motor car engineer, 21, that he belongs to the group of Swedish Speedway riders who afford some

Tommy Nilsson (Getingarna)

The legendary Ove Fundin

promise for the future. But the real breakthrough has yet to come as far as he is concerned.

Indianerna ('the Indians', meaning American Indians) are newcomers to the All-Swedish Division this year. They are turning up with a very good squad with as foremost members the World aces Bernt Persson and Hasse Holmquist. This team also comprises Sven-Erik Andersson, a construction worker, 23. Sven-Erik last year surprised everyone by taking the Swedish Junior Championship, in tough competition. Then he proceeded to help his team to enter the All-Swedish Division in the qualifying race against Kaparna. Göran Pettersson, a tinsmith, 18, is another rising star created by the Indianerna on their own. A lot still remains

Dackarna team-mates Stefan Johansson (left) and Ake Anderson lead Smederna's Ake Dovhead (2) and colleague Gote Nordin at Malilla

One of Sweden's most loyal servants Soren Sjosten with one-time Belle Vue team-mate and double World Champion the late Peter Craven.

for him to do and the 1974 season will, perhaps, tell what are his real capabilities.

Well, this is a list of the would-be ace stars of the future, on whom special training is bestowed, in Division 1, the way Swedish Speedway is looking today. In Divisions 2 and 3 there are obviously some riders with good capabilities but they will hardly be able to show what they are up to in just one season. As it is now, Sweden has a variety of clubs and competition is therefore becoming progressively tougher over the years and, as a rule, it takes some three to four years for a rider to attain a position of international standing.

And those with international qualification in Swedish Speedway have already made themselves a name on British tracks in the course of the years. Regrettably, they will not be making their way back there in 1974.

Swedish Journalist LARS EDGREN is editor of his country's top motor-cycle monthly *ALLT OM MC*.

(*Translation by Swedish Technical and Export Translation Company Ltd.*)

3

HEAD HUNTING FOR FAME
by Peter White

Speedway is a *world* sport.

Its frontiers extend from the sunny climes of Australasia to the frozen wastes of Soviet Russia. No other sport, with the possible exception of soccer football, reaches such vast global dimensions. And new outposts are being added annually. For the speedway connoisseur this is the era of ever-expanding horizons.

The roar of racing motorcycles is now common to such diversified countries as Japan, Africa, Scandinavia and America. Now another frontier has been added to the fold. A new and exciting outpost reminiscent of romantic novels, adventuresome jungle tales, rolling drums and head hunters.
New Guinea.

For the first time in history the shattering blare of straight through exhausts and that so-distinctive smell of burning alcohol has reached the tropical highlands of this obscure Down Under territory, a territory which is still struggling towards civilization in the modern world.

But in the picturesque village of Granville at Port Moresby right now it's a struggle of a different kind: to foster sufficient equipment and competitors to emerge on the world speedway scene. And all associated with world speedway are anxiously casting eyes in the direction of this obscure, but excitingly unique, outpost in the hope of seeing it cultivated to take its place on the international stage.

The possibility of speedway in New Guinea originally evolved from the dreams of a young Australian who was working at Port Moresby in early 1971. Alan Page was driving a rally-cross car at the only venue for sporting cars in the district—run by the South Pacific Motor Sports Club—and decided that an active speedway circuit to cater for solo motorcycles and sedan cars could be a viable financial proposition.

Page began looking around for a suitable site which he soon found: a natural ampitheatre about three miles from Port Moresby's Jackson airport. The land was held under lease by a now-deceased Chinese businessman, Mr. Luk Poi Wai, who became interested in the project and agreed that a speedway could be built on the location selected. An access road into the area was constructed using an old war-time track as a basis and the actual racing track soon began to take shape. The track itself was carved out of the bottom of a natural basin which resulted in an earth-retaining wall acting as the safety fence. This effectively reduced the initial cost of setting up the track. Advertising signs were added to the surrounding area, grass-roofed sun shelters built for spectator comfort and a concrete and glass control tower-cum-broadcasting box was constructed.

Presto . . . the new speedway was ready for its inaugural meeting.

And so in mid-1971 speedway came to New Guinea.

On a balmy tropical Sunday afternoon a crowd of 2,000 people witnessed the opening ceremony which was performed by the Lord Mayor of Port Moresby, Councillor Oala Oala-Rarua.

Ringside view of the Port Moresby.

Grandstand facilities rank with Wembley—or do they?

Racing was held fortnightly on Sunday afternoons for the remainder of 1971 and throughout 1972. Fields consisted of stripped road bikes and moto-cross machines and sedan cars. Racing was controlled by an enthusiastic band of fairly knowledgeable speedway enthusiasts.

Late in 1972 Page left Port Moresby to return to Australia and control of the Granville speedway passed into the hands of its present promoter, John Gombos. Gombos is a successful sedan car driver at the speedway, having pushed a much-modified Australian Holden Torana car to many victories. In 1973 Gombos took a big plunge and installed lights, not the usual overhead lights as found at most Australian and European speedway tracks, but a series of steel pylons around the perimeter of the track fixed with quartz-iodine floodlights.

The span of light from each just overlaps its neighbour and provides an accurate ribbon of light around the racing arena. Similar lights illuminate the pits, spectator and parking areas . . . and also the infield which accommodates trail bikes which race in moto-cross and steeplechase events between speedway races.

Night speedway was an immediate success, running fortnightly on Saturday evenings. The programme consists of speedway bikes, moto-cross, sidecars and sedan cars. A few brave souls are currently constructing midgets and it seems that fans will soon be treated to the sight and sound of the spectacular Americanised speedcars in action. The sedan cars have gradually evolved into a collection of well-prepared, very fast smaller vehicles like Toranas, Datsuns and Minis.

During 1972 Marshall Paull, a prominent scramble and short circuit rider in Port Moresby for Honda and Suzuki, imported an ex-Ole Olsen grass track Jawa and proceeded to race it at Granville speedway. It was an immediate success and Paull was soon giving the 250 c.c. and 350 c.c. roadsters of his contemporaries long handicaps and catching them in the four laps of the quarter-mile circuit.

Later the same year John McDonald, a former Port Moresby go-karter who had left to reside in Australia, returned with a 500 c.c. JAP which he had raced occasionally at the Tralee speedway, Canberra.

The duels between Paull on the Jawa and McDonald on the JAP were highlights of those early speedway days in New Guinea. When McDonald left again for Australia he sold the JAP to prominent sedan car exponent Ian Mc-

Port Moresby teenager Francis Vains leads ex-World Finalist Jim Airey on his home track.

Donald (no relation) who soon had his son Kevin, a keen scrambler, taking up the challenge against Marshall Paull. Kevin soon outgrew the old JAP and a new Jawa was purchased from Australia. Kevin McDonald quickly proved that the Jawa was an excellent acquisition by winning several solo finals in succession. Meanwhile his JAP had been purchased by Mrs. Barbara Roach, wife of former South Australian stock car driver Ron Roach, who put her 14-year-old son, Marc, on it after a short training period. Marc at that time was riding a hot 125 c.c. Suzuki in scrambles and short circuit events.

Another youngster, 15-year-old Francis Vains, had commenced to ride Marshall Paull's Jawa in solo heats and was showing tremendous promise. Then motorcycle enthusiast Ray Lewis purchased a Jawa from Jim Airey in Sydney and put young Vains on the bike. That gave New Guinea four speedway bikes: three Jawas, one JAP.

Kevin McDonald proved master of the bunch with Francis Vains finishing ahead of Marc Roach on the lower-powered JAP on most occasions, and then Marshall Paull.

The biggest thing to happen to New Guinea speedway was the visit to Port Moresby in mid-1973 of star Aussie rider Jim Airey and his proteges from the Harbour City of Sydney, Jim Gosson and Dennis Alderton. Airey turned ou remarkable feats of skill and control and went over very big with the enthusiastic patrons.

Airey, Gosson and Alderton competed in the first-ever New Guinea Speedway Championship . . . which Airey convincingly won from Francis Vains and Kevin McDonald. And for the local teenager Vains to edge such experienced Aussie riders as Gosson and Alderton (who rode in England with Peterborough in 1972) out of the placings at that early stage of his career speaks highly of his future potential. All three of the local youngsters are now mounted on Jawa machines as Roach purchased an ex-Bill Landels bike which the visitors had taken to New Guinea with them.

With the young 'uns improving ride by ride and regular visits by prominent Australian competitors seemingly assured, speedway in New Guinea looks forward to a decidedly increasingly healthy future.

PETER WHITE is Australia's foremost speedway journalist and a regular contributor to Australia's premier magazine *REVS Motor Cycle News* and other world-wide publications. He is also involved in the administration of Sydney Showground—one of the world's most famous tracks.

4

SZCZAKIEL - THE CEMENT MAN FROM OPOLE
by Ian MacDonald

In a small workshop adjacent to the speedway pits at Opole's compact stadium there is a large wall poster. The writing is in Polish of course, but the message is plain and to the point. It reads: JERZY SZCZAKIEL—CHAMPION OF THE WORLD.

Now that certainly doesn't infringe any Trades Description Act—at least not since his controversial victory at Chorzow in September 1973. The only trouble is that the poster has been in its place of honour since July 1971!

Jerzy, it seems, has been the champ for three years. Opole fans will claim that this is true. The poster presented by the local Kolejarz club, was in appreciation of Jerzy's efforts in the 1971 World Best Pairs final when he, together with Andrzej Wyglenda, demolished some of the sport's leading exponents.

Contesting the meeting were stars like Anders Michanek, Ivan Mauger and Barry Briggs. All went under the axe. Szczakiel and Wyglenda rattled off six consecutive 5-1's. Both Poles recorded scores of 15 paid 18.

The meeting was held at Rybnik. Home country advantage was cited as a probable reason for the Poles' dominance but it must be remembered that this same Rybnik track was the scene of Britain's first Test win in over thirteen years in Poland last year.

The Poles won. Wyglenda was superb. But Szczakiel, the young 21-year-old from the cement area of southern Poland, was the real giant that day.

1971 was a good year for Szczakiel—at least it was until the closing weeks of the campaign. As the shutters came down on the season Szczakiel was a sad and disappointed man. He had felt exactly the same the year before. He felt rebuffed by his own speedway hierarchy.

It was almost a case of history repeating itself. In 1970 the Kolejarz team were getting their first taste of Division One racing. They did well and finished third in the table. Szczakiel was largely instrumental along with team mate and friend Zygfryd Friedek. Szczakiel had his sights firmly on the world championship. It was scheduled for Wroclaw and with domestic qualifying rounds only, he fancied his chances of grabbing one of those six magic places available to the host nation.

As the final rounds drew close Szczakiel was one of the in-form candidates. He clinched a final spot, but was withdrawn by the authorities. His place was taken by Friedek.

By rights Szczakiel should have been the main threat to Ivan Mauger's hopes of a world final hat-trick. As it turned out Mauger mesmerised the Poles, Friedek broke his arm, and Szczakiel had a broken heart. What should have been the biggest day in his short career was, instead, a tragedy.

Szczakiel has always been a quiet, serious introvert. The events of September 1970 did nothing to bring him out of his shell. However, Szczakiel was a fighter. He was determined to prove he was really one of Poland's top riders. He ached for a chance to show his worth.

The opportunity came at Gorzow which was the scene of the Polish Riders' final. Szczakiel was razor sharp in practice. He was first to the tapes for his opening ride. He exploded from the traps, swept into the first turn and . . . parted company with his machine!

Fifteen minutes later he was back in business. He had swept to two brilliant wins and really opened up the chase for the title. Fourth time out he was well in command when his bike spluttered to a halt. He finished with eight points and a lot of new supporters. He had missed glory in 1970 but he was still a youngster and there was always 1971 . . .

Szczakiel was determined that a world final place would not be denied him this time. The final was to be held in Sweden. The main threat to his dream appeared to be the venue for the European Final. It was that notorious graveyard of East European speedway hopes—the Empire Stadium, Wembley!

Szczakiel was not unduly dismayed by the opinions of experienced Polish riders who said, 'Waste of time getting through to Wembley, you won't get anything there!' Nothing, he vowed, would stop him reaching Ullevi. It looked to be no idle boast. As the season progressed his form became more and more impressive. He proved he could live with the best when he starred in that memorable Best Pairs meeting. He also made his first trip to Britain. The Poles didn't enjoy much success on the tour but Szczakiel had no complaints. He scored points at tracks where more experienced team mates were really struggling.

His one bad moment came in the Test at Leicester when he was largely instrumental in a crash which resulted in injury to Nigel Boocock. It knocked the wind out of the Pole's sails for a while. His confidence took a bit of a dent and he struggled in the next match. But at the close of the tour he was again looking like the Pole most likely to become the country's new number one.

The Poles returned home. Szczakiel grew in stature. He reached the European final along with Jan Mucha and Henryk Glucklich. Now came the big test. Could he ride at Wembley?

The answer was 'yes'. He won his first race, went on to notch seven points, became the highest scorer outside of British League performers, and was through to Ullevi. Szczakiel seldom shows signs that he has a sense of humour. He is essentially an off-track thinker. But after the Wembley success he let the mask drop briefly when he 'admitted' that things had gone exactly to plan. 'I realised that my first outing was the easiest on paper,' he said, 'I was walking round Marks and Spencers in Oxford Street the day before the meeting when I decided that I would stake all on that first race.

'I was not interested in second place in my opening race, for there was no guarantee that I would do any better than third in any of my other heats. It had to be three points at the start or nothing.

'I came to the tapes, they went up, I closed my eyes and flew.'

Szczakiel's bubble burst a couple of weeks later when he finished last in the world final. 'I didn't ride at all well,' he admitted. 'Perhaps I should have closed my eyes!'

However, he was the only Pole to reach Ullevi. Not a bad achievement. Certainly one that should have put him on something of a pedestal with the Polish authorities. A gold medal from the Pairs final and a world final place deserved some reward.

But it was not to be. Two big meetings remained; the World Team Cup at Wroclaw and the Polish Riders' Final at Rybnik. He was favourite for the home title and considered one of the big guns for the Wroclaw meeting.

The afternoon of the World Cup was sunny and the stadium was packed.

But Szczakiel was again a sad and disillusioned man. The Poles were in their familiar scarlet race jackets with the silver eagle. Szczakiel, however, lent against the pit gate wearing jeans and a light blue windcheater. He had been dropped from the side. The Poles hottest property had been given the grand order of the boot!

The Poles were shattered that day. They virtually surrendered as Britain, in magnificent form, and the Russians, ground them into the Wroclaw dust. Had Szczakiel been there Polish pride would almost certainly have had one lifeline. In the space of twelve months Szczakiel had experienced two great moments of success and had suffered two crushing body blows.

There was still the Polish Final and the 'forgotten man' was odds on to win. Even the threat of a suspension after he had barged Jan Mucha into the fence in a match against the Russians broke his concentration for the big Rybnik encounter.

Tragically in his first race he was dreadfully boxed at the first turn, had to shut off to get out of trouble and could do no better than third. From then on the meeting belonged to the Opole star. He smashed the opposition out of sight. Four races—four impeccable victories. Unfortunately his final tally of 13 points put him one behind eventual champion Jerzy Gryt. But, at least, he had made his point. A fact that the press, still seething from the Wroclaw debacle, were quick to seize upon.

Szczakiel spent a great deal of time in his workshop during the winter. The poster on the wall was a constant reminder that he could, and had been, a winner of a major speedway event. Perhaps at this time he was as near as any rider has ever been to giving it all away.

He carried on. He was rather subdued at the beginning of the 1972 season. He was winning races but the spark that had characterised his style in the previous year was missing.

The season wasn't that old when Opole met Zielona Gora in a league match. Zbigniew Marcinkowski fell in front of Szczakiel and both riders were taken to hospital.

Physically, Szczakiel was still in near perfect shape but the accident brought on a rather severe form of nervous anxiety. He missed a great deal of the year's racing. He was dropped from the senior group of riders and instead was entered for the Junior Championship—a competition that he had won, incidentally, back in 1969 when he was in only his second season of league racing.

The Poles entertained the Swedes for a Test series. The matches came and went. There was no sign of Szczakiel. Suddenly he popped up near the end of the series in the Test at Czestochowa. The Swedes were tracking Michanek, Lofgqvist, Persson, Bengt and Tommy Jansson, and Tommy Johansson. But Szczakiel, the last minute inclusion, was the master. He scored a superb 17 ... not bad for a rider who had just finished as runner up in his country's Junior Championship!

By now Polish speedway had undergone quite a change. Established giants like Woryna, Wyglenda and Waloszek were fading. Whizz kids like Jancarz and Glucklich were beset by injuries and dropping out of the running. The world final was again scheduled for Poland and all eyes were on the latest sensation— Zenon Plech. Plech was the best bet, so everyone fancied, to combat Mauger, Michanek and Olsen.

Szczakiel? Surely not in with a real chance. He had missed the boat, or had

The style of the 1973 World Champion.

Jerzy Szczakiel

A future Polish World Champion—that's what many forecast for Marek Cieslak.

been forced to miss it, back in 1970. He wasn't the star anymore. This view was reinforced by his poor showing in the British-staged World League. He failed to score and returned home prematurely when news of his mother's death reached him.

Szczakiel had again been dealt a rough hand. He went through the motions for a few weeks. He reached the world final almost unnoticed. At the official practice he was regarded as a no-hoper. In fact he was so bedevilled by nerves and a mammoth loss of confidence that he was physically ill. For the third time it looked as though he would be hauled out of a major meeting.

The authorities relented. He rode in the final and he became the world champion. The speedway world was shattered. The Poles were embarrassed. Would he prove to be a good champion? He had a chance to answer this a couple of weeks later when the World Cup was held at Wembley.

He was on a hiding to nothing. His head was really on the chopping block.

Two more of Poland's brightest prospects, Ryszard Fabiszewski (left) and Andrzej Jurczinski (right).

He had a disastrous week in London. He wrote off his bike in practice, was instrumental in an injury to team mate Mucha and capped it all, on borrowed machinery let it be said, by failing to score in the meeting. His reputation was swept away in one night's racing.

The Poles refused to allow him to accept bookings in Britain and Australia. A pity this, as he would probably have flown around those Aussie circuits. In fact he wouldn't have been able to go anyway as he caught pneumonia and was out of action for the remainder of the season.

But the record books are there for all time. He is the world champion. He may not be the best rider in the world, he may not be the best rider in Poland but he did beat 15 of the world's top men at Chorzow.

He came back from obscurity to snatch something which it seemed too many forces were hell bent on denying him. It may have been luck on the night but it wasn't luck that got him there. He has overcome a few tragedies in his short life and that takes a certain courage. The word 'Champion' can take many forms.

The man Jerzy Szczakiel beat to take the 1973 crown . . .

5

ALPHABETICALLY SPEAKING

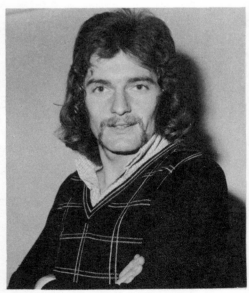

Josef Angermuller (Hull)

John Boulger (Cradley United)

Neil Cameron (Wimbledon)

John Davis (Oxford)

Ken Eyre (Wolverhampton)

Odd Fossengen (Poole)

35

David Gagen (Kings Lynn)

Ted Howgego (Ipswich)

Bengt Jansson (Sweden)

David Kennett (Hackney Wick)

Ulf Lovaas (Oxford)

Charlie Monk (Halifax)

Bengt Norregaard (Denmark)

Jon Odegaard (Norway)

Zenon Plech (Poland)

Tommy Roper (Hull)

Jiri Stancl (Czechoslovakia)

Ian Turner (Kings Lynn)

Zenon Urbaniec (Poland)

Bob Valentine (Sheffield)

Ray Wilson (Leicester)

Bob Young (Rye House)

6

SEVENTY SECONDS OF ACTION

by Mike Patrick

Australian Carl Askew had an unwanted reputation as one of the wildest recruits to Second Division racing in 1974 and his hairy style often saw him on the wrong end of a race exclusion.

Test match action with Belle Vue's Peter Collins leading Swedes Bengt Jansson and Tommy Petterson.

Division Two action again with Sunderland pair Brian Havelock (left) and Russ Dent leading veteran Clive Hitch at Rye House.

Big-time sponsorship has come to speedway in recent season . . . and with it top-class excitement. 1974 World Final reserve Tommy Jansson leads colourful Chris Pusey (Belle Vue) in the Daily Express Spring Classic at Wimbledon.

World Championship action—this time from the 1974 British semi-final with winner Dave Jessup (Leicester) fighting off the challenge of Newport's Phil Crump and, in the background, Kiwi Bruce Cribb.

Excuse me—do you mind if we play footsie! Birmingham's George Major dances around Rye House's Clive Hitch whose aptly named partner Brian Foote heads towards the fence.

It's that man Peter Collins again . . . this time on the outside of Sweden's Kenneth Selmosson and Belle Vue team-mates Chris Pusey and Soren Sjosten who are, on this occasion, rivals and not partners.

More footsie . . . this time its 1973 British Champion Ray Wilson hopping past Hull's Bobby Beaton in an early season World Championship round.

7

THE FIRST OF THE KIWI GREATS

by Ivan Crozier

New Zealand has produced three world champions—Ivan Mauger, Barry Briggs and Ronnie Moore. But to anyone brought up on New Zealand speedway there was another man who would have been the world's number one if he had not retired prematurely. That man was the great Geoff Mardon. Here, New Zealand writer Ivan Crozier—a former rider himself—pens a tribute to the first of the Kiwi greats.

Geoff Mardon may be remembered by a lot of people for a lot of things in his relatively short career as a top flight rider. But by most followers he is the man who pioneered more 'firsts' than anyone else.

He was the very first New Zealander to gain a place at the World Final at Wembley. After a dramatic run-off with Olle Nygren, Mardon's third place paved the way for a flurry of placings for New Zealand that seems to want to go on for ever. That night he was very much an outside prospect. Fellow Christchurch rider, 20-year-old Ronnie Moore, had come close to taking that historic spot with fourth place in the two previous years, but 1953 was a milestone for New Zealand speedway and it was Geoff up there on that tractor.

It all started back in Christchurch at the now defunct Aranui cinder track. Whatever it was about that circuit that produced so many of the super-stars it had its magic touch layed heavily on Mardon. He was swept up in the post-war speedway fever that gripped the city and established each rider as a hero parallel only to Hollywood. It had to be experienced to be appreciated. In no other field at the time, from rugby to aviation, did the public admire as the distant demigod, the speedway rider.

Geoff was a leg-trailer. There were a lot of leg-trailers there at the time. He tried hard and pranged in the most spectacular fashion. The year was 1949. Speedway was young and there was no overseas influence to up the grade.

After the first two summers Aranui had begun to get a regular floating population of riders, not only from the other N.Z. centres, but England! At last the styles of pre-war dirt track began to vanish and youngsters like Moore and Mardon progressed away to a slicker style that stayed with them and only needed polishing up on their arrival in England.

Ronnie went on with his tutor Norman Parker to join the Wimbledon Dons, and Geoff joined forces with his mate Trevor Redmond at Aldershot. The year was 1951. Suddenly the 24-year-old Kiwi was a professional. He had sold up everything he owned—his carpenter's tool kit, his road bike, his speedway bike, everything. All he possessed was a home-made set of leathers cleated and padded like the Michelin man, and a burning desire to do well for Third Division Aldershot. Willing to smile at misfortune but shy and withdrawn from those he didn't know well, he displayed force and aggression on-track to bring the stands to their feet and behind him to a man.

Living in digs with Redmond—even sleeping in the same double bed—and depending entirely on track earnings to pay the thirty bob a week board and keep his half of their 1934 Chrysler going, did not seem all that difficult when expenses were low. But nothing is that simple. Within a month of arriving he broke a collar bone and was sidelined. His earning power was curtailed and in a very short time with a little simple addition, he realised that he was not going to eat . . . that he had to get back, broken bone or not.

'It was the most difficult thing in the world', he recalls. 'It took all my energy to keep weight off my left arm . . . slowly it would slide off the handlebar and droop. Race after race and me trying to earn a quid and get that useless hand back on the 'bar . . .'.

The World Championship round at his home track, Aldershot, that year was a disappointment for him. With only ten points he was out of the running and seemed unable to progress to the next round. However, he did get a reserve position and luck was on his side. He was called up to ride at Oxford and Leicester and grabbed at the chance.

At Oxford, against the likes of Jack Young, he scored eleven points and then came one of the greatest thrills of his career—he won the Leicester meeting with fourteen points. Next man home was his old buddy, Trevor Redmond.

After the depressing ten points at Aldershot to this! And into the final round against the crack riders of the senior division . . .

The unknown Kiwi from an obscure Third Division track appeared at Wimbledon and New Cross, tracks he had never ridden before, surrounded by names that were legends when he was hammering in nails six months ago in Christchurch. The subtle atmosphere of professionalism, cool efficiency, swamped by the very history of his surroundings. The shy Mardon groping for a friendly face in the pits was a complete lie to the urgent, skilful performer on the track. At Wimbledon only Split Waterman and Ronnie Moore could hold him and he finished with twelve points.

Where's my name asks Geoff Mardon after winning the 1954 Brandonapolis.

On the tiny New Cross bowl he quickly found that his fervour was getting him nowhere and settled down to finish with nine creditable points, and was the first Third Division rider to get this far, even though it was only as second reserve on the great Final night of 1951.

This was a magnificent first season for Mardon. Not only had he been selected for a place in the first ever N.Z. Test team, but in the League average table he held fourth place with an average of ten points a match—300 points in all and seven paid maximums.

Naturally his brilliant performances had come to the attention of First Division promoters and just before the season ended Mr. Ronnie Greene opened negotiations for Geoff's transfer to Wimbledon. A transfer fee of £1,050 was agreed and the unknown Kiwi became a first division star in his own right.

Buddy Fuller had arranged an unofficial tour of South Africa by Trevor Redmond 'and friends'. Geoff, with Scot Jock Grierson, decided to accompany Trevor. The money wasn't the greatest but by all accounts it was an unforgettable experience.

'We arranged to fly out from Stansted', recalls Geoff. 'It was one of Fats' historic arrangements. Five times we set out from where we were staying at the Moore's before we at last got going. There was this great four-engined Avro Tudor that looked like a Blenheim Bomber . . . The first time there was a wing off—the next a couple of engines out—the next something else spread around the ground getting fixed. When we did get going one of the ground crew pointed out of the window at a burnt-out wreck lying alongside the control tower and said that that was the other half of William Dempster Airlines—a Pole had pranged it not long before.

'Well this Avro lumbered off and stayed on full throttle for three-quarters of an hour before being able to ease back. I actually timed it—and its ceiling was only 500 feet. When we got over Africa we had a great view . . . everything was so close. Just didn't have the guts to go any faster and get up. And if we wanted to go forward we had to step over a dirty crate of gold bullion—right in the passageway. I can still see Fats Redmond staring at the gold through the slats with a dazed look on his face.

'Anyhow, we arrived safely in Tunisia, although it was close in Paris when the old girl ran right to the end of the runway, just cleared the last wire fence and began to sink back to earth again. Jock got down on his knees, kissed the ground and swore he'd never fly again. We returned on the same plane, but true to his word he sailed home!'

The rarer atmosphere of Johannesburg's 6,000 feet left the JAPs lifeless and the Overseas troupe had no answer to Henry Long and his Nitro-methane. Fuller arranged to introduce speedway to entertainment-starved Durban and brought along the Johannesburg riders plus a couple of the overseas men. The track was 250 yards and it was of course at sea level.

'The meeting was due to start at eight,' Geoff told me. 'At six the place was chocker. You couldn't get a cat in. The gates had to be closed. Well, Buddy was elated. He'd been really worried about the publicity—you know, whether he'd done enough or not.

'The Johannesburg riders lined up. They now had a lot lower gear and all the power because they were at sea level. Up went the tapes and they all reared and sat on their bums. The crowd never made a sound ... just silence—no reaction, and the riders all sitting there on the track looking at each other. Well, away they went again—started their bikes, reared, and flipped again. There they were, just as before. No reaction from the crowd, nobody stirred. You got the impression that they were waiting for the next trick, or something.

'By this time Buddy was starting to panic and appealed to me to do something—anything to get a reaction from the mob. So Buddy and I rushed out and did an impromptu match-race. We cut each other up something awful. I knew it looked pretty frightening.

'When we finished and came to a stop outside the pit gates we began to throw punches with straight faces—the crowd began to stir. Then Buddy gave me a bit of a push and I stumbled back into my bike and fell right over it with the bike thumping down on me. The crowd exploded. They jumped the fence and rushed us. We had to get a police escort out of the stadium. And I still don't know who they were after—me or Buddy ...'.

While in South Africa Geoff injured his shoulder and lost all feeling in his left arm. 'You could put a cigarette out on my hand and I wouldn't feel it', he said. This injury could have been the end of his career had not he come across one of the finest surgeons in the world. This surgeon was a German-Jew and the top man in Munich before the war. He had just managed to escape Hitler's anti-semetic purges and settled in that one corner of Africa where Geoff found him.

Back in England, and after a shaky start, Mardon began to climb the charts of the First Division. Paired with Moore in a best pairs Festival Trophy competition on the Wimbledon track, the two cleaned up. By the end of the season he occupied tenth place in the League, scoring 321 points for a match average of 8.6 points. Well-established, and living better than the set-up he and Redmond had suffered, he nevertheless was known as a hungry rider and guested almost as much as team idol Ronnie.

D

The World Championship rounds saw him out of the running failing at Norwich, after picking up a handy ten at Wembley. His impressions of 1952: 'It was a long time ago and costs were low those days and a bloke could earn a quid—and hang on to it. There was a lot to learn and I had to catch up on all those riders that had reached Division One after years of campaigning.'

At Belle Vue he came upon a rider with a reputation for vigorous riding— Dent Oliver. Mardon was unimpressed by reputation but decided to keep a good look out, and then in the heat of riding promptly forgot. He recalls diving into a corner and having Dent arrive under him with a load more forward motion on than expected, and purely by accident impaling Dent's front wheel with his handle-bar, ripping all the spokes out and seeing Oliver loop over the top of him. He gained a lot of respect from this one accidental encounter.

With the season over many Australasians returned home to the still-existing post-war boom. Geoff and Brian McKeown were snapped up by a hard pressed Canterbury team. Both Ronnie and Barry Briggs had joined Dick Campbell and organiser Trevor Redmond in South Africa and left Canterbury short against the British-strengthened Hastings, Dunedin, Wellington and Auckland centres. Mardon proved unbeatable on his old stamping ground, Aranui. It seemed by those old programmes that all the might of England's greats descended on him to stop his run. This was the greatest one-man show south of the equator and nobody could do a thing about it.

Nearing the peak of his short career he returned once more to England and Wimbledon. His form held and he qualified for the World Final with eleven points at Wimbledon and thirteen more at Belle Vue, being beaten only by Ronnie Moore and Louis Lawson. This total of twenty-four points saw him safely through at last.

Nobody fancied his chances on that historic evening in September of 1953. Here gathered together was the cream of the world's speedways and nobody with so little experience stood a chance. Ronnie, who had just decided that once and for all he was going to ride for New Zealand and not Australia, was generally thought an average prospect after a fourth the year before, but not his mate Mardon.

But Ronnie fell in his first race and Mardon won it! So with a boost like those three points Geoff progressed through the night to amass twelve points and equal third with Olle Nygren. This was his, and New Zealand's, greatest hour. And no one was going to take that third spot away from him.

The run-off between the Swedish champion and the Kiwi was a boomer. Mardon riding as cool as a veteran held off the wildly challenging Nygren, eventually crossing the finishing line a brilliant winner, for the Swede had tried every trick he knew to get by, falling in a last desperate bid on the final bend. He had achieved it. Before 93,000 people he had put New Zealand on the map.

The season of 1954 was Ronnie's first win in the Final. Geoff qualified again with 24 points but was out of the running.

Team-mates at Aldershot in 1951—Geoff Mardon (left) and Trevor Redmond who still retains an interest in speedway as the New Zealand team manager.

The news was out that Geoff was to marry Valerie, Ronnie's sister, in December of that year on his return to New Zealand. To round off the season he won the Brandonapolis from a star-studded field, including the new World Champ himself.

After the wedding in Christchurch he and his new bride began to get themselves organised for the return trip to England and a new season.

Said Geoff: 'We had most of the gear packed away and had our tickets when I turned to Val and out of the blue asked her if the whole thing was worth it. Just didn't seem right dragging a wife half way around the world . . . and her having lived on the move with her parents involved in carnivals all her life. So we just unpacked everything and I sold my four bikes, my leathers and everything, just like that, and retired.'

Ronnie had retired a matter of weeks before and suddenly Wimbledon and New Zealand were without two-thirds of their heat-leader strength. Barry Briggs alone began to take up the hunt for world honours.

Four years passed. The Mardons took up life in suburban Christchurch, he building a house and starting a business and Val looking after Jill and Jacki, born in 1956 and 1958. It was a good life and Geoff dabbled a little in scrambles, but nothing serious. He and Les Moore even built a sports-car special.

Then came an offer from Aranui to have him ride in an 'Old Timers' race. Amused and keen to put on an act Geoff organised leathers and a bike, but was

A Best Pairs partner—Brian McKeown, now one of New Zealand's leading race officials.

taken ill with kidney trouble and had to withdraw. But the excitement of the preparation stayed with him and after the operation he discharged himself from hospital on a Saturday morning, arrived at Aranui that night and discovered the South Island Championship was about to be held.

He entered it on the spot and won it from Ivan Mauger and Brian McKeown! He was delighted. His times were right up to scratch and everything felt great.

The last meeting of the season, a week later, was the final night for Aranui Speedway. The famous bowl had been sold for housing development. An historic night. Barry Briggs, the then World Champion, with Geoff, Brian McKeown and Ivan Mauger put on a series of events called the International Best Pairs and Geoff won the very last bike race of Aranui's history.

Ronnie was top of the tree again in England but this time it was Briggs who was making retiring noises. Southampton cabled Geoff hopefully and were overwhelmed when Mardon accepted and returned once again to the British Speedway scene.

His first-night tally of eleven points, even though tiring, in the latter stages, set the seal on his come-back. Top scorer for his team within four matches, he consistently ranked amongst the first half dozen. With the World Championship round weeks away—and this his last tilt—he broke his jaw but continued on to qualify. Again with twenty-four points, he began the evening well with five points for two rides but was unplaced later in the programme. But he was there to see brother-in-law Ronnie take the title with seeded champion **Briggs** coming in third behind Ove Fundin.

Rival and brother-in-law Ronnie Moore.

It had all happened. He had returned and was often a better rider than before his retirement. Now a greater tactician and at the peak of his career he retired from the British scene and returned home to take up, with Les Moore, sports car racing. He and Les carried on for some time with the Moore's 'Wall of Death' routine.

Geoff had set himself well and had a taxi to drive when not working for Les or away following the sports-car circuit. As he very soon became one of New Zealand's top-flight drivers it would seem that speedway had lost him for ever. But the urge was still there.

He was approached to ride against the Australian Test team at Western Springs, Auckland. Borrowing a bike from Merv Neil he competed with success— gaining maximums in his two outings in the three stage test—and won the N.Z. Championship at which the Australians were also competing. Since then, Geoff has had the occasional ride at Templeton and despite more big offers from England, a recent eight-lap trial at Templeton has convinced him that he is 'too old' for speedway. There was still car racing.

Geoff went into temporary retirement after Les Moore was killed while competing in their Special. Later he drove the famous fire-breather Stantion Special and had a lot of fun and won a string of trophies before the car became outclassed. George Begg offered him one of the exotic single seaters that bore his name and again came the successes, as sure as clockwork. Then it was all over again, he won a thirty-lap feature event at Ruapuna and announced his retirement from competitive motor sports.

He said at the time (March 1971) that he would strive at golf and aimed at a sixteen handicap. He is now a sixteen handicap player and one wonders as we watch him tinkering with his son David's scrambler what this remarkable man will turn his eye to next.

8

J.S. HOSKINS~ THE WAITARA WARRIOR

Author, Playwright and Promoter Ian Hoskins writes a tribute to his father

New Zealand, one of the most far flung outposts of the former British Empire, has played a unique role in the history of speedway racing throughout the world. Quite apart from producing a trio of world champion riders who have dominated the international scene since 1954, the land of the Kiwis and Canterbury lamb gave birth on April 16th, 1892, to a man who was destined to become the pioneer of the sport of speedway itself—my father, the great Johnnie Hoskins.

Johnnie, who was born at Waitara, a small town with a Maori name in the North island of New Zealand, also had as his birthright the astrological sign of Aries the Ram, the fiery symbol that has given rise to such diverse pioneering personalities as Adolf Hitler and Charlie Chaplin. Charlie in fact was born on April 16th, 1898.

My father's early formative years were typically wild. He took on anything that came along and one of his first jobs was that of a sausage skin maker in a packing factory. 'I had to remove the smell from the intestines of the sheep before they could be used on the sausages.' He told me. 'I lost more friends that way than any other kid in town. I was the original big stinker.'

He soon tired of this self-imposed unpopularity and later took a job in the local post office which was to shape his future for many years ahead. In those days, telegraphy was the main means of communication and Johnnie took to it with a zeal that bordered on the fanatical. He practised the morse code day and night until he became a very efficient operator. This was the skill that in future years he was able to put to telling use in two world wars.

Recalling his early days in New Zealand, a country by the way in which he has never once promoted a speedway meeting, he was reminded of the time when he almost disappeared from the face of the earth without a trace. 'It was possibly the closest I have ever been to an early death,' he commented.

He and a young friend, Jack Burnard, went horseback riding on a hunt for wild pigs one day at Otorohanga, and the chase led them to the entrance of a cave in the side of a massive cliff. Their curiosity aroused, they armed themselves with a lantern and candles and went inside. After exploring deeper and deeper into the cave, the lantern gave out and they realised to their horror that they were completely lost. Unaware of the dangers of potholing, they followed the course of an underground stream, often stumbling in it up to their necks. 'We must have been going for a couple of hours in pitch darkness, and for all we knew, the stream we were following could have been going down in circles underground.'

Fortunately, they came upon a pin point of light in the distance and finally emerged, shaken and saturated, on the far side of the cliff a mile or so from where they had entered. Never again did he venture into unknown caverns, but adventure continued to dog his energetic footsteps. Well before he was twenty, Johnnie decided that he had to go to Australia and he spent his savings on a boat trip which landed him in Sydney without a penny in his pocket.

He immediately headed for the nearest post office where his skill as a telegraph operator sent him on a posting to Wagga Wagga and later, to Tambo in Central Queensland. After a six hundred mile train journey from Sydney, Johnnie arrived in Tambo by stage coach after a bone shaking sixty mile journey.

He spent over a year in Tambo where, among other things, he was elected as the secretary of the local hearse committee. It seemed that the only hearse the town owned had collapsed while carrying a coffin across a creek and funds had to be raised to buy a new one. He was even offered the chance of a partnership in a massive sheep farm near the town, but as he knew next to nothing about sheep and as the owner's daughter had been casting matrimonial glances in his direction, he decided that his future lay elsewhere.

Johnnie returned to Sydney where he met a cousin of his who owned a butcher's shop. He was immediately welcomed into the business and seemed set for a new career when the pony that pulled the delivery van he was driving one day slipped and damaged its forelegs. His cousin blamed Johnnie for the accident and when his wife appeared upon the scene brandishing a broom, he again took off in a hurry.

He decided this time to head for Port Darwin in the Northern Territory of Australia because he had heard that there was a shortage of telegraphists in the town. He boarded a ship for the long journey and found himself in the company of no less a person than His Excellency, the administrator of the Northern Territory, Doctor Gilruth, a New Zealand born man of Scottish extraction.

His Excellency informed Johnnie, as the journey progressed, that there was a young German upstart on board who rather fancied himself as a boxer. He enquired if Johnnie knew anything about the noble art of self-defence as he would dearly like to see someone have a go at him in the ship's gymnasium. Having been reared in the hard school of rough and tumble, Johnnie agreed to meet the German although he had never before put on boxing gloves in a ring. Fortunately for him, he K.O.d his rival in the first round and immediately won the friendship of the Doctor, a man who helped him considerably after their arrival at Darwin.

Darwin, as it turned out, was a town of destiny for Johnnie. It was there that he was able to demonstrate his skills as an organiser and learn the techniques of sport promoting. When war broke out with Germany in 1914, he joined the navy, but because of his knowledge of telegraphy he was made a Chief Petty Officer and attached to the staff of the wireless division in Darwin. He worked the overland telegraph line to Adelaide and also helped operate the naval cable system. Darwin in fact, was the most important telegraph and wireless station in Australia and quite by chance, Johnnie was on the receiving end of one of the most dramatic episodes of the entire war in that area.

He happened to be on duty one night when he picked up a radio signal with a very strange note. It had obviously come from out at sea and he surmised that it might have been from the *Emden*, the notorious German cruiser that had been sinking Allied shipping in the Pacific for years undetected. 'I passed the message on to Melbourne where it met with top priority. We took it in turns listening out for further signals and from their strength we could determine how far from Darwin the ship was lying.'

Not long afterwards the *Emden* sunk and as the very first telegraphist to have located her, Johnnie felt that his war effort had been amply rewarded. He also recalls one of the highlights of another side of his war exploits, that of entertainment officer to the many sailors who used to put into Darwin for shore leave.

Over the years he had staged cycle racing, boxing shows and all manner of diverting events including wrestling. He had in fact, built up a very useful string of wrestlers that numbered a huge Scot, a powerful Russian, several dinkum Aussies and a sixteen year-old Darwin lad who was looked upon as the local hero.

Accordingly, when the cruiser *Encounter* arrived in port after seeking the *Emden*, Johnnie approached Commander Burrows on board with a challenge to match his sixteen year-old lad against any boy his own age on ship. The bout would take place in the local stadium and would be supplemented by several ship v. shore boxing matches.

The Commander decided it wasn't worth the trouble removing all the wrestling apparatus ashore for just one bout. There had to be two contests or none at all. 'Not realising what I might be letting myself in for, I accepted the arrangements on the spot,' said Johnnie. 'However, when I returned to inform my lads that I wanted a volunteer to wrestle the *Encounter's* second nominee, a certain Leading Seaman Oakey, the champion of the entire Australian navy, they chickened out to a man. I had no alternative but to agree to make up the number myself.'

What ensued was a salutory lesson for all would-be wrestling promoters. The local stadium was packed to capacity by the crew of the *Encounter* and local residents of all nationalities. In the opening bout, the local sixteen year-old had defeated the ship's first nominee and the sailors were thirsting for revenge. Johnnie seized an opportunity to plead to Mr. Oakey's sense of fair play just prior to their entering the arena and the champ promised to take things easy.

The bout began with the sailors goading their hero into mayhem. 'Kill 'im Oakey! Twist 'is ruddy neck!' Johnnie recalls that never in his life has he been given such a run-around. 'Oakey may have been fooling, but he bounced me all over the ring. The crowd loved every moment of it and afterwards I asked Mr. Oakey why he hadn't lived up to our little arrangement.'

The champion replied that Johnnie had looked a bit too fit for his liking and he didn't want to take any chances. 'Somehow, I didn't *feel* so fit after he'd gone,' said Johnnie, 'and ever afterwards I vowed to remain on the right side of the spotlights, the ringside, not the ring.'

As Johnnie's showmanship abilities became accepted, he took on the organising for the Red Cross charity funds and one day he was invited to run a baby show. 'I'm sure there has never been a baby show to compare with this one,' he observed.

It seems that the mayor of Darwin was a communist and not very popular, but he fancied his chances of winning the baby show and entered his child immediately the contest was announced. Johnnie then decided that in order to induce as many voters to back their fancies at threepence a go, he would track an outsider into the running.

'I approached a Mr. Cheong, one of the leaders of the considerable Chinese community in Darwin and told him to enter one of the Chinese babies. As the white vote was bound to be split over the dozen or so white babies, all he and his friends had to do was vote solidly for their own entry and the chances were they would come up with a winner.

'Naturally, if news of this had reached the ears of the mayor, I stood a chance of being run out of Darwin on the seat of my pants,' added Johnnie. 'It so happened that my prediction came true and I will never forget the moment, in the crowded grounds of the Governor's mansion when the mayor stepped up to proclaim the winner, silver trophy at the ready. As he opened the slip of paper with the name of Mary Ah Wong duly enscribed as champion, his eyes almost popped out of his head. His announcement of the verdict brought the house down.'

His Darwin days were soon to end, however, and the end of the war saw him in charge of the wireless station at Mount Gambier. He then retired from the service and returned to Sydney where he became involved in journalism and photography for a while before becoming interested in the health and naturopath craze that had swept Australia in the wake of Bernard McFadden, the famous keep fit therapist.

After performing a near miracle cure on a woman who had written to him complaining of almost every illness under the sun, he headed north up to Queensland again where he did a three month tour on horseback before shipping himself out to the wild islands of New Guinea.

His New Guinea experiences alone would rate a book. He tells of one story of his stay in a native village when he foolishly invited one of the tribesmen into the hut he used to develop films. As the native gazed into the developing dish he was given the surprise of seeing his own photograph suddenly 'coming to life' before his very eyes.

The man's expression of awe changed to one of terror. 'You debbil debbil man!' he cried and fled from the hut. An hour later, Johnnie found him lying outside his hut in the village, his eyes rolling wildly. There had been many cases in New Guinea of natives lying down and willing themselves to die. Seeing this, Johnnie decided that this man was his personal responsibility and he stood over him with a stick for twelve solid hours and threatened to beat the living daylights out of him if he dared to give up the ghost.

It is often said it is better to be cruel to be kind and the choice of facing Johnnie Hoskins with a stick, or taking a chance on a heavenly banana plantation, was an uneven contest and the man lived to tell the tale.

Another time he met up with a tribe of head hunting cannibals and even entered their sacred burial grounds in a cave to take photographs. He managed to escape the angry natives by the skin of his teeth. On another occasion, he went down to a beach for an early morning swim. He noticed that one part of the beach was netted off and he naturally assumed that this was the safe area and dived in.

After a few minutes of splashing around, he observed a Chinese running madly down the beach towards him waving his hands and yelling for him to come out. He had just seen a huge alligator enter the water. Only later did he learn that the nets were used as a fish trap and when the tide went out he realised he had been swimming blissfully among sting rays and other lethal fish in addition to the stray alligator. That was probably why my father became a fatalist. He is inclined to the view that what is to be will be, although he is not above giving fate a push when opportunity comes along.

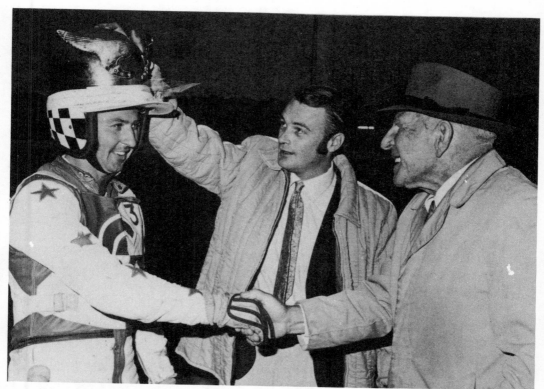

Johnnie Hoskins congratulates Australian Lou Sansom—returning to Britain in 1975—on retaining his Silver Helmet while Lou's Workington promoter Ian Thomas touches the helmet to make sure it really is silver.

From New Guinea he returned to Sydney and from there, on another of those intuitive hunches, he bought himself a one way ticket for West Maitland for absolutely no reason he could think of at the time. He arrived broke to the world and within minutes met an old friend who put him in touch with a contact that led to him becoming the manager of the West Maitland Showground.

It was in Maitland that he met and married my mother and it was there that he first introduced motor cycles to the Maitland Show. This was in November, 1923 and it was from that historic date that the sport celebrated its fiftieth anniversary meeting at Canterbury speedway in Kent last October. Just for the record, I was born in West Maitland in 1924, the eldest of three sons, and so the story goes I was taken to my first dirt track meeting at the age of one.

With Maitland established, Johnnie opened a track further south at Newcastle and this was a tremendous success. He then moved on to try his luck in Sydney, a city that had never proved a happy hunting ground for him in the past. His venture at the huge Sydney Royale track cost him a lot of money. In fact, it was there, years later when he returned to Australia with a team of British and Australian stars, that he featured in the most hair-raising track incident of his career.

'What happened was this. In England we had become used to rolling starts where the starter would stand on the track and wave down the riders until they were all in line and then flag them to increase speed so that they would cross the starting line together. Clutch starts had not been invented.'

Johnnie added that on this occasion, a test match between Australia and England, one of the Aussie riders had been dropped from the team and had created a stink about it in the press. 'Naturally, the public suspected that I was trying to swing the match England's way, although nothing was further from the truth.

'On the night itself, some of the races began to get out of hand at the start. There was false start after false start and I decided I had had enough. So—I stood in the middle of the track myself, and prepared to wave down the riders in the English style until it was time for them to open up and go. The riders, seeing who it was out there, must have decided to give me a rise. Instead of shutting down as they entered the home straight towards the start, they all opened up together and came roaring at me at seventy miles an hour!'

Johnnie added that he was rooted to the spot with horror. As the four bikes roared past, the handlebars of Billy Lamont's machine hit him and sent him flying. Lamont himself went spinning down the track and finished up with his wrist caught in his front wheel. 'Well—the public wanted to kill me!' said Johnnie.

'They thought I had deliberately nobbled another Australian and although only winded, I lay down as if I was dead as the mob screamed for my blood. Fortunately, the riders themselves were able to pacify the public and the meeting continued—but don't talk to me about Sydney!'

In 1928, Johnnie, complete with his family, set sail to try his luck in England along with the cream of the Australian riders. It was there that he met Arthur Elvin of Wembley and an agreement was made to introduce the sport to the Empire Stadium in 1929. What followed has never been fully appreciated by the sports' historians. With the vast Wembley canvas open to his ideas and his personality, he created the guide lines on how the sport should be presented.

Many of his ideas were later adopted by other professional sports. He was the first to think of team pennants for motor cars. He created a massive supporters' club; he had speedway's first mascot, war cry and team song. The pattern of his Wembley presentations have hardly varied over forty years.

More than this, Johnnie later advocated the idea of having a world championship competition based in Britain. It took him three months of hard persuading and arguing before the other promoters voted it into a reality. As a reward, it was agreed that West Ham would always have the first qualifying round in the competition, as this was the track he was running at the time.

Whatever has been said about my father, no one can ever accuse him of not thinking 'big'. His ideas were always grandiose. Who else could have dreamed up the idea of promoting speedway at Wembley on a Tuesday and a Thursday in the same week and also promoting a meeting at the Monjuich stadium in Barcelona on the Sunday in between! And this was in the days before air travel was commonplace. Apart from the cross Channel section, the entire journey had to be made by train. It went on for months!

Unfortunately, the Elvin-Hoskins association broke-up and he returned to Australia with a team of British and Australian star riders. He then took a party of riders with him to Canada and America. They landed in Vancouver and finished up in New York. Unfortunately, he was the right man in the right place at the wrong time. It was the era of the great depression and sport was the prerogative of the gun-toting thugs spawned in the days of prohibition. He couldn't beat the gangsters in New York and he refused to join them despite running a number of meetings at Coney Island.

The family then returned from Australia to England after an absence of one season. Johnnie took over West Ham, a track in the east end of London. This was possibly his greatest hour in speedway. Always the champion of the underdog, he turned an ailing promotion into a smash hit. He gave speedway fans

Always a shrewd businessman J. S. H. sold Barney Kennett to First Division Hackney Wick for a then record fee of £2,000 and one penny!

a sixpenny 'gate'. He recruited forty thousand supporters and held them in a constant state of speculation as to what they were going to see next.

Everybody in speedway before the last war still talks about West Ham. Where his showmanship instincts had been soft-pedalled at Wembley in order to conform to the 'tone' of the venue, at West Ham they were given free rein. To a pop-eyed public he gave them elephants, camels, racing cheetahs, glass coaches pulled by white horses. He even gave them royalty when the Duchess of Kent graced a charity meeting he put on. Every week he came up with something new and something the fans did not expect.

His style of promoting has always been unique. There has always been more of the Chaplin in him than the business man. His theory was that speedway racing was an aspect of show business and that the very worst thing to happen was for *nothing* to happen during a meeting. That is why he was called 'Roaring John'. The moment there was a delay between races and the public began to fidget, off he would run to the pits, his arms waving like windmills, his voice yelling blue murder. Woe betide the poor rider who dragged his feet without good cause.

'If you went to see a play at the theatre,' argued Johnnie, 'and there were constant breaks in the performance, you would soon lose interest. When I used to go storming into the pits at the speedway, the public at least knew that some-one was doing something about the delays. It was all a big act, but it got results.'

When West Ham came bottom of the league, Johnnie capitalised on failure by having a huge symbolic wooden spoon presented to him. He followed this up by having tiny wooden spoons cast in metal to hang on the badges of the supporters. He even gave West Ham a white track when he imported hundreds of tons of 'silver sand' from Cornwall. I remember seeing huge maps of England and Australia drawn upon the white track surface in red ash prior to a test match between the two countries. What an innovator!

It took Adolf Hitler to put a stop to British speedway in 1939. The family lived at Wanstead at the time in a typically large house. With his source of income dried up, Johnnie gave his services to the Air Ministry as a civilian wireless instructor. He was posted down to the Yatesbury camp in Wiltshire where he helped train thousands of budding air crew.

In 1945, with the European war at an end, he straightaway plunged back into speedway promotion at a new venue for the sport at Odsal stadium in Bradford. The fact that Odsal had a capacity of over a hundred thousand, albeit on the rim of a vast bowl of ash, made him all the more attracted to it. He also ran meetings at Newcastle and Glasgow White City in the same year, two tracks he had opened before the war.

Bradford was another huge success when the First Division was restarted in 1946. For years the crowds never fell below twenty thousand for a meeting. Unfortunately his personality clashed with that of the stadium owner and he was obliged to sell out in the early fifties. This proved to be the apex of his promoting career. He lost a great deal of money by promoting the Ashfield Giants team in Glasgow. The stadium had to close with an average gate of seven thousand spectators! This, of course, was in the days of huge entertainment tax on speedway. White City, Glasgow, followed suit shortly afterwards in the great speedway depression of the 'fifties.

Undaunted, Johnnie was invited to manage Belle Vue in Manchester and here again he made an unforgettable impact. He introduced stock car racing there and it is still going strong as one of the greatest venues for this type of sport in Britain. After many years at Belle Vue where he also handled the publicity, he parted company in the 'sixties to re-open New Cross speedway in London.

This was short-lived due to his being unable to track a competitive team and he turned to Harringay and stock car racing which became another smash hit. He still held interests in Scottish speedway of course, at all the tracks I opened there in the 'sixties, I gave my father a half interest in return for having taught me the promotorial business at White City when I came out of the R.A.F. in 1946.

In 1967, Johnnie returned finally to his first love when he opened the Canterbury track in Kent. It was there that he celebrated his eightieth birthday and in 1973, at the final meeting of the season, he proudly staged the fiftieth anniversary meeting of the sport he began at West Maitland in 1923.

This year, 1974, he celebrated his eighty-second birthday. He still has the energy to dig the garden every day and grow his own vegetables at his beautiful cliffside home at Herne Bay overlooking the sea. 'If I had been more of a business man than an idealist,' he says, 'I should have been worth a million pounds. I once had the chance of going into the film making business in the early days, but I chose speedway instead. I have never made a fortune, but I think I have made millions of people happy over the years and this to me has made my career more than worth the while.'

Yes—the cinema may have lost another Cecil B. De Mille, but speedway gained a showman who stands indisputably on his own. Herne Bay is a long, long way from Waitara, New Zealand, and one day with luck, he intends returning home to see his many surviving relatives there. It is doubtful however if he will ever promote the sport in the country of his birth—age is the only opponent he cannot compete against on equal terms. He has dreamed great dreams and has lived to see them become realities and he started out with nothing . . . More than that, no-one can ask of any man.

9

CARRYING THE FLAG

by Philip Rising

Speedway has made great strides since the formation of the British League in 1965 and the advent of a Second Division three years later. More tracks means more riders and Division Two has encouraged and increased the influx of young talent into the sport.

Yet of all the riders who have burst upon the scene in those ten years only Ole Olsen has managed to go on and win the coveted World Championship. Ivan Mauger, the dominant figure of the decade, was already riding in 1965, although his first title success came in 1968. Barry Briggs, Ronnie Moore, Peter Craven and Bjorn Knutsson all came into speedway in Britain between 1950 and 1961. And Ove Fundin, the most successful of them all, made his bow during the same era.

It would appear that quantity has taken the place of quality. So many who began with a flourish and showed rich potential have failed to reach the very top. The path to the World Final has got progressively harder, of course, and Mauger has set a standard and a pace that none, not even Olsen, have been able to match.

There is evidence, however, that England, Poland and Sweden can lay claim to having young riders who could become worthy world champions in the not too distant future.

The most obvious candidate is Peter Collins, whose achievements over the past couple of seasons stamp him as a rider of outstanding promise. His rise to stardom has been meteoric and, with his 21st birthday still to come, he has a wealth of experience behind him.

Peter started riding motorcycles when he was eight years old! Bill Collins, head of a family of motorcycle enthusiasts, built Peter a scaled down James

E

Peter Collins—England's white hope   *Sweden's bet Tommy Jansson.*

machine and he rode it round fields at Partington near Manchester. About the same time he became a follower of speedway and there was never any doubt in his mind that, one day, he would ride for Belle Vue.

By the time he started speedway at the age of 16 the precocious Peter Collins had already made quite a mark at junior grasstrack events. He attended the Belle Vue training school in 1970 and was with Rochdale a year later after a few second halves at Crewe.

The late Maury Littlechield maintained that Peter should have become a Crewe rider. Peter himself insists that he never had thoughts of riding for any track other than Belle Vue and it was in 1972, aged 18, that he became a member of the senior squad at Hyde Road. He helped Aces win the First Division championship that year and, 12 months later, was British Junior Champion and a World Finalist. Peter didn't cause any sensations in the giant stadium at Katowice but he learned much that will stand him in good stead in future World Finals.

It was in England that Collins really hit the headlines. His clashes with Anders Michanek became the major talking point of the season. There was that controversial run-off for the International Tournament trophy at Wembley when Michanek came under Collins and was adjudged to have caused young Peter to crash. A few weeks later they met at Belle Vue in the final of the Speedway Star Cup and again it was Collins who took the honours, despite riding with a hand injury. In the World Team Cup Final, again at Wembley, he scored a maximum.

During the winter he toured Australia and, briefly, New Zealand, and continued to pile up a string of impressive performances. All this before his twentieth birthday. It's no wonder then that Collins is hailed as a future World Champion . . . but so have many others before him and still we wait for a rider to bring the trophy to England for the first time since Peter Craven's last success in 1962.

It would be fitting if Collins follows Craven. Belle Vue was Craven's home for so many brilliant years; the initials are the same; and there are many similarities in their riding.

Collins has tremendous natural ability and races a motorcycle as though he really loves it. His temperament is ideal. He doesn't seem to suffer from a complex about big occasions—some riders do—and has supreme confidence without being brash or arrogant. His equipment is good and his motors, looked after by Guy Allott (shades of Mauger and Olsen here), ensure that he has fast, reliable mounts. He had a spell when eagerness at the gate cost him a few exclusions but, as his confidence has grown so, too, has a belief in his ability to come from the back if the need arises.

Peter is a sensible lad who has kept his feet firmly on the ground despite all the adulation that has gone his way in the past few months. His family background will help, too, and he seems a steady, mature sort with the right ambitions.

If England looks to Peter Collins to take over the mantle formerly worn so magnificently by Peter Craven, then Sweden will look in the direction of Tommy Jansson to succeed Ove Fundin.

Fundin won his fifth championship in 1967. Since then the Swedes have been without a World Champion and not even Michanek, with his impressive riding in the British League and early rounds of the championship in 1973, could break the duck.

Michanek was one of the favourites for success at Katowice. After all, he'd won the European Championship and the British/Nordic Final . . . and he even had a British League average better than that of Mauger! It appeared that '73 would be his year yet, on the day, he cracked. After trailing in fourth in his first ride, he broke the tapes in another and was a mere mortal when so many expected him to join the very top bracket which is still shared only by Mauger, Olsen and Briggs.

Tommy Jansson was only reserve that grey afternoon and again this year. Two years before he had reached the World Final in Gothenburg but finished without a point. His record in international competition, highlighted by victory in the World Pairs with Michanek in 1973, is not exceptional.

Why rate Tommy so highly? Because he has a certain class and magic quality that few can match. His experience to date is limited. He had half a dozen matches for Wembley—all away incidentally—and was then released. The following year, 1972, with Wimbledon anxious to strengthen a struggling side, he was brought back to England.

Tommy was an instant hit. He immediately took to the Plough Lane circuit, with its tight corners and hidden dangers, and started to build up the sort of following that put him on the path to taking over from Ronnie Moore as the idol of the Dons supporters. Pretty soon he was scoring almost ten points per meeting but it wasn't so much the scores as the manner in which he collected his points that earmarked Tommy as a rider with a true champion's pedigree. His fast, stylish riding contains some characteristic Swedish flair and improvisation and these qualities rapidly endeared him to speedway folk everywhere.

At the end of the 1972 campaign he jetted off to Australia and spent several months lapping up the sunshine in between turning in some jet-propelled performances on the big Aussie tracks. It was ideal experience and Tommy himself has always maintained that he needs as much racing as he can get.

Unfortunately things haven't turned out well for him. His 1973 season in England was cut short when he was called up for his period of service in the Swedish Army. Shortly before he left Tommy produced a string of brilliant displays, including one memorable 15-point maximum at Swindon. When he returned home to don his army uniform he had a British League average of well over 9.00 points . . . not bad going for a youngster in only his first full (or what should have been full) season.

There are one or two question marks about his ability to reach the very top but his faults are of the type that can be quite easily rectified. Barry Briggs, for example, recognises Tommy's inborn skill but feels that on a bike Tommy lacks the necessary 'thrust and drive'. Says Briggo: 'Tommy's got lots of ability but strikes me as being a bit like Bengt Jansson—not hard enough.'

The ban on Swedish riders who couldn't meet certain guarantees has cost Tommy Jansson his place in the Wimbledon team and, without regular competition in the British League, it is doubtful whether he will progress sufficiently to make his presence really felt in the World Championship. It also remains to be seen whether a spell in the Army has made Tommy more self-reliant. There was a feeling at Wimbledon that he tended to lean on other people too much; even that he was a little spoilt. There were those who suggested that, if he had a bad first ride, he'd crack.

Personally I think there was a little truth and substance in what was said. But, Tommy is young, inexperienced and if he has such faults then time will rapidly iron them out. What really matters is his prowess on a speedway bike and there can be no complaints there.

Poland's answer to Collins and Jansson is undoubtedly Zenon Plech, 21 years old and a superstar already. Zenon was branded as the wonder boy in 1973 and the rider most likely to uncrown Ivan Mauger but I don't honestly think the Poles were as confident as some others seemed to be.

As it was the unfancied Jerzy Szczakiel defeated Mauger and became Poland's first ever World Champion. Szczakiel proved the best rider on the day, and you cannot take that away from him, but you can hardly mention him in the same breath as Mauger, Olsen or Briggs. But for a last ride crash, largely through no fault of his own, Plech would have been in that run-off with Ivan and Szczakiel. I have always maintained that Ivan would have done better had Plech joined his countryman in the race.

But that's another matter. Plech lost—or was robbed of—his chance. He'll get another. Briggs again: 'Plech would be World Champion within three years if he rode in the British League. As it is I'm not so sure.'

Plech made a deep impact when he came to England with the Polish side for the International Tournament. He had already shown what he could do in the World Pairs Final and his reputation as a spectacular, full-throttle merchant was established for him.

Poland's second match was at Oxford. Plech had an almighty prang in his first race and didn't ride again that evening. A few days later he drew admiring glances from Mauger and Briggs when riding against New Zealand. And he was superb at Hackney against England on a track made sodden by heavy rain.

Plech had done enough to confirm his status as a rider with a bright future ahead of him. Predictions about him taking the World crown were, however, a little rash and premature. Obviously he had a real chance on a track in his own country. And none doubted his ability to beat anyone, Mauger, Olsen and Michanek included. What was clouded in suspicion was whether he could put together five top class races without making some sort of mistake along the way.

Plech's chances of becoming champion in future years were enhanced by his two months in Australia, New Zealand and America with the World Champions troupe. He gained valuable experience of different tracks and learned a great deal from spending so much time in the company of Briggs and Mauger.

Personally I'll never forget his riding in Houston. He was brilliant in practice and on the first two nights when the riders gave exhibitions. He gives the impression that he would ride all day given the chance. He doesn't worry about the bike he rides, as long as it goes, and that sort of attitude must work for him. He doesn't

A pensive Zenon Plech.

have hang-ups about different handlebars or things like that. During the actual Astrodome meeting he'd ridden well and the crowd were taken with his spectacular bursts round the outside. It was important that he win his last ride. 'Ivan's bike,' he said to Barry Briggs and promptly walked over to Ivan's place in the pits and pointed to the Mauger machine.

'Sure,' said Ivan and out went Plech to ride a race that gave me as much pleasure as anything I've seen. He came from last to first with sweeps round the outside and cut-backs to the inside that defy accurate description. And all on a bike that he had never ridden before.

During the course of one meeting in New Zealand the incredible Plech rode five different bikes. He has a marvellous phlegmatic approach and phenomenal skill. Whether being restricted to racing in Poland will hold him back remains to be seen but there is no doubt in my mind that he is destined to take his place in speedway's Hall of Fame.

He was a relative late starter in the sport and has no great record as a motor-cycle enthusiast. But once he started riding speedway in Poland he rapidly made great strides and before long was eagerly talked about as their white hope for the future.

He gave the impression of being a bit wild and thoughtless in those early days but many felt that, in fact, he was more controlled and a great deal shrewder than people gave him credit for.

However, his extensive trip across the Pacific certainly taught him throttle control, or as Briggs puts it 'that you don't always have to have the gas full on.'

Barry happily relates tales about Plech's riding on the tiny 180 yards circuit at Costa Mesa. He didn't much like the look of the place at first and was very timid and reluctant at practice. But in the meetings he just went out and screwed it on, blazing round with the motor screaming.

'Unbelievable,' says Barry, still chuckling at the memory. 'Even when he's in trouble he keeps going.'

Given regular competition against the best riders, and that means partici-pation in the British League, Plech would be a must. As it is, with Jansson out-lawed, Peter Collins must be the best bet for not just winning the title once but also following in the path of Ivan Mauger and Barry Briggs.

Time will provide the answer and it could well be that some other rider will overtake one of these three. Somehow, though, I doubt it.

PHILIP RISING is a staff writer for the mass circulation weekly magazine *Speedway Star* and business manager of four-times World Champion Barry Briggs.

10

Peter Oakes takes a look at the Ice-Racing Scene and decides it is...
SPIKES, SPIKES AND MORE SPIKES

Picture, if you can, four riders looking like refugees from one of those American tv films about grid-iron men.

Now think of the pencil slim frame of a speedway rig—all bone and little flesh. Put them together like pieces in a jig-saw set and a background of ice and snow. Add in a sprinkling of danger . . . a dash of excitement . . . and the whirring of hundreds of tiny spikes attached to the tyres of your motor-cycle. And somewhere amongst that little lot you have a sport that is unique: speedway racing on ice.

The purists have abbreviated its collective noun to ice-speedway and throughout the months when the sun beats down hard on Bondi, Manly and Glenelg beaches the madmen of Eastern Europe zip around speedway-shaped ice rinks indulging in one of the strangest motor-cycle pastimes of all. It is difficult to describe the action as it is something completely divorced from any other form of motor-cycling even though it is a blood brother to conventional speedway on a shale or granite surface.

The very nature of the track itself demands a completely different riding technique and probably the most valuable part of a rider's apparel is a piece of tyre that he cuts and straps onto his left knee which replaces the conventional speedway star's steel boot as the point of contact with the track.

The machines they all ride—at a distance—look pretty familiar to anyone who has wandered around the pits at Coventry, Melbourne or Costa Mesa, save for a spiney guard that covers the front and back-wheels.

It protects hundreds of razor sharp spikes that are seated into the tyres, front and back, to aid traction on the slippery surface. Regulations state that each machine must be fitted with no fewer than 280 of these venomous weapons—each

1974 Ice Race Champion Milan Spinka takes former champion Gab Kadyrov on the inside in the race that decided the title.

of which must be at least 28 mm long. With more than 200 of them on the back tyre you can imagine it isn't the most genteel of sports and injuries are generally of a serious nature. In this year's World Final, for example, Czechoslovakian Jan Verner was carted off to hospital where surgeons inserted 40 stitches in a leg wound.

Closer inspection of the ice-racing machine—basically there are three makes on the market: the all-conquering Jawa which comes out of the same workshop as their speedway and long-track machines; a Swedish-built Ricksson; and the German Geigenbach which has still a long way to go before it can challenge either the Czech or Swedish machinery—throws up several other less obvious

Hardly a spike between them as Russians Boris Samorodov, Vladimir Zibrov and Gab Kadyrov show their brilliant skills on ice.

73

modifications.

While the ice-racing engine is only 500 cm³ it has a two speed gear box with foot change—first gear is used from the tapes and it is knocked into second going into the first turn—and the machine has a longer wheelbase than a conventional speedway steed with telescopic front forks and a steering damper. Like a speedway bike it is rigid at the back and this year a new rule was passed demanding that every machine be fitted with an ignition cut out which is wired up from a button on the forks to a cord around the rider's wrist.

In the past, it seems, out-of-control machines have caused untold damage,

Pre-meeting parade and time for a chat for Russians Vladimir Kotchetov, Alexander Stcherbakov and Boris Samorodov.

necessitating the new ruling which is also in force at conventional speedway in Sweden.

Prices for a new machine are astronomically high by European standards—an ice-racing rig complete will cost over £1,000 compared with the western price of £490 for a speedway machine. A second hand Ricksson, though, brings the price down to around £400 which seems enough for the beginner to pay!

Usually the ice-racing engine has a higher compression than its speedway—or long track—counterpart, although a balance has to be reached to prevent lopping at the start.

Despite the expense of getting started on ice (remembering that most of the Iron Curtain riders are mounted on state or club-owned machines) it doesn't seem to restrict the number of riders willing to have a go. Instead for the British rider there is a more serious handicap than either injury or expense: the lack of training facilities.

Oxford's Richard Greer—a competitor in the last two world championships —summed it up: 'To train I have to go to the continent. That's why I'm thinking of packing it up. If we could use a speed-skating rink in England for practice I'm sure I could go quite well and the same goes for other English riders.

'I'm sure too that it would catch on in England if only there were the facilities and tracks.'

One little-known fact is that it was Kiwi Ivan Mauger who became the British Commonwealth's first ice-racing challenger!

Back in 1967 the Russians were given FIM permission to stage their own World Ice-Racing Championship. There was only one problem: so few competitors came from outside the Soviet Union that they were forced to invite riders from other nations—to give true credence to the World Championship tag. Not surprisingly they wanted a couple of British riders included in the line-up even though they knew—and everyone else knew—that no one in Britain had seen an ice-racing meeting . . . let alone ridden one.

But the enterprising Russians offered to cover the expenses of two riders and a team manager. Mauger, then riding at Newcastle and spending his Southern Hemisphere winter in Britain, heard of the offer and, never one to spurn a challenge, he made official application to the Speedway Control Board to be in the team!

Chatting one night with his Newcastle team-mate and fellow Kiwi Goog Allan—a steady but far from top-grade speedway rider—who lived a few doors down the road, he talked him into becoming the British number two! Effervescent extrovert Trevor Redmond—one-time rider but by then a promoter—was also interested and accepted the job as team manager. So the British party comprised three New Zealanders.

It sounds simple to talk about riding in the World Ice Racing Final in Russia but Mauger and Allan faced a nightmare trip to the qualifying round at Novasibersk. After flying into Moscow they then spent a couple of days sight-seeing before boarding the Trans-Siberian Railway for a 55-hour train journey to the final venue.

Machines were provided by the hosts for the two Kiwis and Mauger had a typical ice-racing debut . . . he fell off in practice!

But he can give some insight into the art of ice-racing. He says: 'One really imagines ice-racing as something absolutely fantastic and an incredible spectacle but in fact it is nowhere near as exciting to watch as regular speedway.

A superb shot of an ice-racing machine— in the hands of Britain's Richard Greer.

'I was first out in practice and I know I wasn't going very fast but I was enjoying it. As I came back in a Swedish friend, Evert Andersson, gave me a few points saying I wasn't getting the bike down low enough and that I was to almost touch the left handlebar on the ice as I went into the corner.'

The four-times speedway champion took that advice: but when his handlebar touched the ice the front wheel lifted and he lost all adhesion . . . skidding into the ice barrier that surrounds all the tracks.

Despite their lack of experience the two Kiwis were through to the semi-finals (their first involvement in the sport at any level!) and while Mauger had terrible problems adjusting to the less spectacular style of riding Allan was a revelation and scored seven points in his first ever meeting!

He didn't qualify for the final—being held in Moscow—but returned to Russia the following year with a new partner and was well placed to make his final debut when he was involved in a nasty crash that saw him spend a week in a Russian hospital with a busted collar-bone!

A sign that the championship was becoming a little more representative of

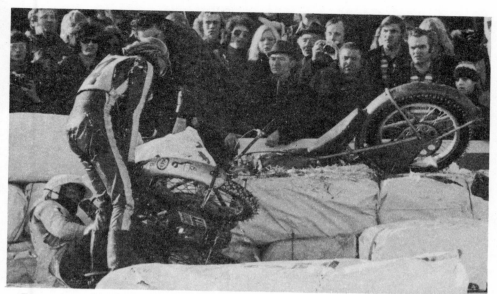

Excuse me—could I have my bike back! Bertil Dedering helps Roelot Thijs out of a tricky spot . . .

Getting grip at the start—that's Czechoslovakia's Stanislaw Kubicek.

the world was that qualifiers for the 1968 final included four Russians, three Czechoslovakians, a couple of Swedes, a racing pair from Finland, two East Germans, a sole West German, a Bulgarian and a gentleman by the name of Shalbugin from Mongolia!

Despite the presence of eight nationalities in the final—and several others in the qualifying rounds—the ice-racing scene was dominated by the Russians with their only worthwhile opposition coming from the Czechoslovakians with Sweden—who have run a league competition for some years—probably ranked third in the world. Outside those three countries no other nation could field a representative four-man side in those early days, but as the seasons have passed so the standards outside the Soviet Union has improved.

Despite the lack of practice in Britain—to date there has never been an official ice-race meeting held in the British Isles although there has been talk of trying to arrange one in Scotland on the Aviemore resort site where the management also own Belle Vue speedway—in 1970 Andy Ross became Britain's first World Finalist.

Ross, a scrambler of note who later switched to speedway with some success before retiring after breaking his leg, had accompanied Goog Allan to Russia in 1968 and was so taken with the sport that he was to wear the Union Jack on his body colour for some seasons.

Pioneer Allan (ranked by the Russians as eighth or ninth in the world at the time of his crash) is one of the few authoritarian voices on ice-racing behind the Iron Curtain as he travelled extensively watching league and individual meetings as well as competing in the World Championships.

Explaining the techniques of a still mysterious sport he told me: 'In ice-racing you don't broadside at all. You have to get both wheels inline all the way.'

This differs from racing on shale although in essence the theory is correct—that the first rider with his wheels in line is usually the fastest.

However the crucial point is that on speedway you can let the back wheel drift away without losing too much ground—in ice-racing it is a fatal mistake that soon sorts out the novices from the star men.

'You have a steering damper tightened so that it's very hard to steer and first time on it is rather like riding a bicycle with the wheels locked,' explained Goog.

The throttle technique, too, differs from conventional speedway when you often have to wind it on going into the turn. In ice-racing you NEVER turn it on going into the turn—always waiting until you are half way round the bend.

Gating, too, requires a slightly different technique. Despite those lethal spikes on the back tyre it is terribly easy to spin on the starting line and too much throttle sees the back wheel ripping up the ice. Too little and the front wheel lifts high into the air in a spectacular loop the loop. The secret then is find the right mark on the throttle—and stream into the first turn with the front wheel about six inches above the ice.

As a first-time visitor to ice-racing the sheer spectacle of a new sport appealed. The glistening white of the snow and the ice added a new dimension but as a journalist I still find it hard to write of the purple line instead of the innermost white line!

The line, marking the innermost track dimensions is usually six to nine inches thick and heaped inside that is four or five inches of snow. The rules say a rider can put his knee over the line—but if both wheels go over on comes the red exclusion light.

While information from behind the Iron Curtain is limited (it is a curious fact that there is no Russian sports paper that gives complete results and often it is difficult to elicit information of conventional speedway meetings in Russia let alone ice-racing) it appears that most tracks have an overall length of around 345-350 metres although they vary tremendously in shape.

Some have long straights; some short straights; some narrow corners; and some wide corners. The biggest stadium in Russia—and oft-times venue for the top individual meetings—is the Moscow Stadium which is one of the smallest tracks in the country, also being used for ice-hockey.

Other notable tracks are at Novasibersk, Kisselevek, Trokopievesk, Temerovo, Sterlicamac and Ufa—birthplace of such Russkie notaries as ex-champion Boris Samorodov and the legendary Igor Plechanov.

Elsewhere on the European continent there are regular meetings in Sweden —where major venues include Orebro, Sala, Vardkasen, Karlstad, and Nassjo where the 1974 World Final was staged—Holland (Assen being the number one track), Switzerland (the famed ski resort of Grenobel), and Czechoslovakia, East Germany and Austria.

Surprisingly one country which seems to have taken no interest whatever in the sport is Poland where one might have expected some of their top speedway names to have ventured over the border to ride in some meetings.

Sweden and Russia stage regular league programmes but elsewhere racing is dominated by individual meetings which add a certain flair and usually ensure a fair proportion of racers adept at the peculiar skills of ice-racing.

Few regular observers believe that a British-based performer could upset the stranglehold that the Russians and Czechs have on the world title although

Huntingdonshire motor-cycle shop owner Andy Ross came uncomfortably close with his fifth placing in the 1970 final—twelve months after making history as the first Britain to reach the final stage of the championship.

Unhappily Ross quit ice-racing after a row with officialdom over cash and withdrew from the following year's competition when he must have stood a fine chance of gaining a place on the rostrum.

Having spent several months riding in as many meetings as possible—including one trip to Canada—Ross was replaced at the last minute and any real hopes Britain had of heralding a breakthrough disappeared.

Australian Geoff Mudge also carved his own little bit of history in the ice when he became the first Southern Hemisphere rider to reach the last sixteen. Bluey—loyal and long-time British league exponent—reached the 1970 World Final but struggled throughout the two days of racing and picked up his solitary point in his tenth and final ride of the competition.

In those days the championship was decided over two days racing and this was the normal formula until this year when it was agreed to stage one sudden death meeting.

John Stayte—a little known Australian who struggled for a place in Peterborough's Division Two side a few years back—is the only other Aussie to have competed in the championship although he fared even worse than Mudgey.

John, a team-mate and friend of Ross, found it so expensive to ride on the ice that he had to sell his machine after competing in one meeting in Germany to afford the fare to return to England!

Other names known to the speedway fraternity the world over include Eric Boocock, buddy Dave Younghusband, Malcolm Simmons, Doug Wyer, Richard Greers and Graham Miles—all of whom have represented their country in the championship.

Beyond the British contingent who are the big stars of the ice-rinks, the riders whose names are as well known to ice-racing devotees as those of Briggs, Mauger and Airey to the shale followers?

No one disputes that the world's leading exponent is Gabtrahman Kadyrov, the 34-year-old Russian who switched to ice in 1964 and since then has picked up six world titles in the eight seasons the competition has had that status. Beatledbrowed Gab hails from that rich nursery of Russian sports masters Ufa and was, at one time, looked upon as a possible threat for the World Speedway Championship.

Until this year when Czechoslovakian Milan Spinka, the Prague policeman who was withdrawn from the Ivan Mauger-Barry Briggs World Champions

Series troupe to concentrate on ice-racing, took over the mantle of the world's number one Kadyrov's main opposition has come from veteran fellow countryman Boris Samorodov who took the crown in 1967. Boris, the tutor of the younger Kadyrov, dominated the sport in the years before it was given official FIM recognition and there is little doubt that he would have run up a long list of World Championship success in the early sixties had ice-racing been recognised by the FIM.

Yet another ex-speedway rider, 44-year-old Samorodov is now approaching the watershed of his career and in recent years has spent more and more time as manager-coach to some of Russia's young future hopefuls.

Beyond Kadyrov and Samorodov it is a little difficult to offer any authoratative ranking of the Soviet ice-men as results from behind the Iron Curtain are impossible to obtain so any non-official judgement would have to rest heavily on performances elsewhere.

And the Russkies are notorious for keeping some of their best performers at home until they consider they are ready to be shown to the outside world.

But judging on world championship performances alone at the head of the queue to unseat the two elder statesmen are Vladimir Zibrov, Sergej Tarabanko, Anatolii Suchow and Vladimir Kotchetov all of whom reached this year's last sixteen.

Beyond these four though is a never-ending list of near unpronounceable names—all of whom could emerge as challengers for the 1975 World Championship crown.

Sweden's chief challenger over the years has been the veteran Kurt Westlund who was his national champion from 1969 until last year.

The heir apparent would seem to come from Bo Kindgren, 28-year-old mechanic Hasse Johansson, Karl-Ivar Wattman, long-tracker Sven Sigurd or Hans Decker.

In Czechoslovakia where Spinka's success has encouraged the sport's rulers to increase the tempo in a bid to unseat the Russians as the number one ice-racing country, Spinka is being feted as a national hero and undoubtedly will play a major part in the destination of future world championships.

His performance at Nassjo—and that of compatriots Zdenek Kudrna (in only his third ice-racing season) and Jan Verner in events leading to the final indicate that there will be an almighty power struggle between the two Eastern bloc countries throughout the seventies.

Beyond those two countries it is unlikely that any other national could take the title unless a future final is allocated to a country where a local man can use his expert track knowledge to good effect.

Even that, though, is improbable as Kadyrov and Spinka have already proved that they can win titles irrespective of the venue.

One thing though seems certain ... the final will never be held in sunny Australia!

11

HOW WELL DO YOU KNOW SPEEDWAY?

Everyone thinks he—or she—knows speedway. But how well do you really know the sport. Below you will find twenty questions, some easy some hard. See how you go on.

To help you some—but only some—of the answers are given in this book so if you want to make it harder for yourself answer the quiz first.

Turn to page(102) for the answers to see how much of a speedway expert you are.

Question 1: Who was America's first ever National speedway champion—and in what year did he win his first title?

Question 2: Which was the first team to win a league title in British speedway history?

Question 3: What does Jap stand for? And while you won't get a mark for it can anyone say in which part of the country the Jap was first manfactured.

Question 4: Speedway was held at Workington before the war. Where was the track?

Question 5: One of these three riders won a pre-war Australian title. Which one? Lionel Van Praag, Clif Watson, Jack Chapman.

The first five questions are mainly for those of you old enough to remember Johnnie Hoskins when he was still a lad. If you can answer them you either have a phenomenal memory or a library of reference books. So let's move onto the post war era—up until 1960.

Question 6: Who won the 1947 Speedway Riders Championship?

Question 7: Son of a Stockholm chemist he joined Harringay in 1951 and has virtually been riding in Britain ever since. Who is he?

Question 8: Who were the Glendale Ghosts?

Question 9: Who were the 1959 National Trophy winners?

Question 10: When did Barry Briggs make his debut for Wimbledon?

Still delving a little too far back in time for you? Let's throw in another ten questions on what has gone on since the formation of the Provincial League back in 1960.

Question 11: In 1960 how many teams contested the National League—and how many the Provincial League?

Question 12: Who was the first Provincial League Riders' Champion?

Question 13: Two finalists in that meeting now have sons riding speedway. Name the fathers—and sons.

Question 14: Peter Craven won the 1962 World Final—who was the only rider to beat him?

Question 15: Who was the first ex-Provincial League rider to challenge for the British League Golden Helmet match-race championship?

Question 16: Cyril Maidment, Sandor Levai, Gordon McGregor and Vic White all rode for the same team in 1965. Which team?

Question 17: Barry Briggs, Geoff Mudge and Don Godden rode together in a European title meeting in 1967. What event did they win?

Question 18: How many teams were there in the inaugural year of the Second Division? And name them!

Question 19: When did Ivan Mauger win his first British Championship?

Question 20: Who was the 1972 Polish Champion?

That's the questions. How good are you? Find out by turning to the answers on page 102.

12

CAMAROS, MUSTANGS, SENCOS AND JAWAS...

by Dave Booth

Very few followers of speedway in Britain and Europe really understand the racing scene as it exists in Australia and New Zealand. But just as the 'down under' countries have over the years inherited a strange mixture of British and American customs, laws and drawls; so too has racing become an unusual mixture of motorcycle and car racing. It is a situation almost impossible to comprehend unless you visit us here and study the situation at close-hand.

To save you the expense then of a thousand pounds or so, let us in this chapter attempt to take you into the Australian racing scene to analyse it, see exactly what makes it tick and to see where it is headed.

The Aussie fan has a unique programme of mixed racing with promoters able to draw from no less than *ten* different forms of speedway racing. Normally a meeting at one of the major tracks will consist of around eight solo, six sidecar, four speedcar, four super modified and three sedan car races—and don't allow that terminology to confuse you for the moment.

So the follower has plenty of variety in his racing. This suits the fanatics who will watch every and any section with interest, but it also develops the 'specialist' . . . it's a common sight to see car devotees arriving mid-way through the meeting and to see the bike fans filing out through the exit gates once their motorcycle events have been completed. Such is the following enjoyed by four wheel sections of racing that even the World Champions' Tournament held at Liverpool (near Sydney) was backed by a couple of car events—just in case all the customers weren't happy with the display of speedway racing.

Yet the tourney fielded the best lineup ever assembled in the country . . . Ivan Mauger, Barry Briggs, Ronnie Moore, Zenon Plech, Edward Jancarz, Ove Fundin and Chris Pusey included . . . who could want for more?

The same, almost inexplicable, situation arises even in Test match or National championship meetings.

This, then, also explains the reason why Australian tracks are very rarely under 400 metres in circumference . . . whereas speedway European style is so spectacular on the squarish, smaller tracks, circumstance has forced Aussie managements to build larger ovals where the cars have enough open space to show their legs.

Remember too that the sport originated on agricultural grounds in Aussie. The tracks around those arenas are invariably used for harness horse racing (trotting) during the local fairs and for this reason they're relatively large. The mixed-fare of a meeting developed . . . now it would appear on the surface that there is no way that the fans will accept meetings featuring only one section of racing.

Three of the leading 'down under' venues—the Sydney Royale, Brisbane Exhibition and Claremont (Perth) operations—remain to this day on Agricultural Fair arenas . . . and they are three of the top half dozen tracks in Australasia.

Just what are the other forms of racing that Aussie followers are offered?

First and foremost there is the highly spectacular sidecar outfit racing, found generally at most centres but exceptionally strong in Sydney and Adelaide. Usually the overseas visitor almost collapses when he takes his first glance at the torrid three-wheel action at either of those centres. And that includes visiting European speedway riders plus American car drivers. They're generally shaken to the tips of their toes!

Aussies for years built up their 'outfits' as they're termed around the old British Vincent HRD motors, but with the parts becoming increasingly scarce many riders are now turning to Japanese water-cooleds such as Suzuki.

I can assure you that the sight of half a dozen sidecar teams tearing around the third-of-a-mile ovals on these $1100m^3$ monsters is one of motor racing's absorbing spectacles. Even the Universal Studios film production crew in Australia to shoot the movie 'The Sidecar Boys' shot considerable footage of dirt-track action after seeing it—even though the original script revolved around road racing.

Speedcar or 'midget' racing was inherited from the United States, where it was all the rage in the late forties (although there had been much pre-war racing). The cars generally are limited to $2500m^3$ power plants (with further restrictions for overhead camshaft motors) over the years many motors have been used successfully but the four-cylinder Offenhauser, because of its torque, has been the most popular choice of the top drivers.

Today, though, the Offy faces the challenge of motors such as the 'SESCO' (basically half a 322 V8 Chevy) and Chevy 11 while the latest experiments are with the incredible little VW units.

Again, the sight of this division on the third-mile (or bigger) ovals can be breathtaking . . . as usually twenty top cars contest a 25 or 30 lap main event. In the 'golden era' of the midget cars in Sydney and Brisbane (the sixties) they were virtually the only section of racing which received any attention at all from the media. They had the tough competition, the following—and the top money. The Sydney Royale, using midgets as its draw and virtually only programming bikes to keep variety in their meetings (and the sections 'alive' in case the car boys started demanding impossible-to-meet fees) drew average crowds of 15,000 for its 24 races.

Even speedway Test matches, which were eventually let lapse for several years, were cut to nine-heat affairs because a full match would cut too deeply into the car side of the programme.

Riders such as Greg Kentwell started their careers in midgets . . . the Birmingham/Harringay 'Blonde Bombshell' of the fifties, Graham Warren, finished his racing days in one . . . even Jimmy Airey at the peak of his career was practising in a midget so that he could turn his attention in later life to where the money was.

Is it any wonder then that Australia produced very few riders of international calibre during that era?

Sedan racing evolved from the English-style thump and bash 'stockcar' racing which boomed in Aussie during the mid fifties—in fact the stockcars still hold the Australian record attendance of 42,000 in Sydney during their first season. Gradually the appeal of a more legitimate brand of hard-top racing won through and these days the American-style 'stockcar' racing—though mainly on dirt surfaces—is extremely popular.

American grand-national sedan racing of course evolved from the prohibition days when the boot-leggers needed suped-up jalopies to escape the pursuing constabulary!

Almost every major Aussie town outside the big cities has a track where sedans, and sedans alone, do their own thing. Cars range from Minis, which are capable of amazing feats with their front-wheel drive, to the V8 Chevy Camaros and Mustangs. Latest development on the down under scene has been the super-modifieds or sprintcars. These units basically came from the sedans and the desire to break away from standard production equipment. Motors are not restricted in any form and they usually look and sound like some form of twentieth century fire-breathing mechanical monster.

Fuel injection, worked-over 350 Chevy V8's, cross torsion bar rear suspensions, quick-change diffs, $80 tyres . . . you name it, these babies have the best running gear you can get—and they go some as a result.

European followers will never see these varied forms of racing in the same manner as the Aussie fans simply because Europe hasn't the racetracks to accommodate them to their best advantage. Even Solo racing itself—or speedway as you term it—is a far different proposition down under.

Teams' racing is almost an impossibility simply because of the distances involved between the major tracks. Last summer a Shield series was conducted between five States but in the main the competition wasn't accepted enthusiastically. Due to the costs involved only four riders were used in each team and the

Australian sidecar champions Gary Innes (driver) and John Lloyd.

whole series was completely devoid of any promotional flair. So it is certain that the vintage programme of handicaps and gate-start races will remain for the immediate future.

The Australian handicaps are a decidedly dangerous form of competition. In six-rider fields, the internationals have to stand the newcomers anything up to 130 metres (for three lap races) or 220 metres for four laps. In other words, don't let anyone tell you that a top, experienced Kangaroo or Kiwi hasn't the nerve and experience to come from behind!

Most tracks limit their books to 18 riders maximum per meeting—the top eight go through two scratch race heats, the top twelve are split into two handicap heats and the bottom six fight out a rookies' race.

In a city the size of Sydney where there are normally around sixty riders actively engaged at any one time, the competition to make the major meeting can be very keen indeed when there is only one track using bikes that week.

For example both Jimmy Airey and the late Gordon Guasco spent many

Saloon car racing at the Liverpool raceway in Sydney.

weeks in the Sydney Royale pits when they first entered the sport as programme reserves before they both received their first ride on a major circuit.

Where then, does the newcomer get his opportunity to break into racing?

Normally he has to pack up and head out of town to a track which might not be able to afford to pay for the topliners and so caters for what is termed Second Division (or B and C grade) riders. There he gets a chance to perhaps beat the bottom eight to twelve riders already on the in-town show. If he can start beating them regularly, he will be given his chance on the city circuits.

Such a 'training ground' is Kembla Grange, 60 miles south of Sydney on the coast and adjacent to Wollongong. Over the past twelve years almost every rider entering into Sydney competition has learned the ropes around Kembla, the country's smallest and slowest track. There the kids can have their falls and spills and are 'blooded' by the time they are thrown into the hard, professional arena of Sydney racing.

Not only is this method of breaking into racing better for the newcomer himself. For the stars, the handicap backmarkers, it lessens the chance of a raw rider falling out in front and bringing down the complete field of six. Crashes in handicap racing can be dreadful affairs as usually the back men are going two to the front man's one.

Other centres, without nearby venues for the beginner, aren't so fortunate.

Most tracks in this position now operate either a series of novice trials or even teams' racing (if you can call it that as the same two 'teams' meet each other every week) prior to the commencement of their meeting proper. This idea though is not popular with show-conscious promotions who only want their patrons to see the *best*. Let's face it, poor speedway cannot help the night as a spectacle and quite rightly the big tracks want to turn their lights on and get into the meeting with a real bang.

It took the Jerilderie Park circuit at Newcastle, 100 miles north of Sydney, to show the others how to overcome that little problem. Jerilderie simply made their track available for practice for competitors each Tuesday night. This idea has had wonderful results in that the area boasts at least half a dozen youngsters coming on in leaps and bounds to perhaps follow in the footsteps of their local hero, Bob Valentine. So the Jerilderie management's investment in the cost of making the circuit available could pay off handsomely.

Once a rider has made his mark in local competition the 'done thing' for him to do in past years has been to pack his belongings together and join the jet-setters on their way to the UK season. Even this aspect of Aussie racing is changing.

New glamour boy of the scene, Brisbane's Steve Reinke, this year won the Australian title from a star-studded lineup . . . yet, for several months resisted the lure of a British League career. Why?

Why throw away a guaranteed income for the uncertainties of English League professional racing . . . particularly with the industrial and living situation that the UK is experiencing at the moment.

Track-wise, the situation is also changing rapidly. Circuits not around the Fairgrounds are being paved from one end of the country to the other to permit improved car racing. Thus either bike speedway racing has to be popular enough in those centres to warrant an additional dirt surfaced circuit being constructed inside the paved oval or the bikes will go completely from their meetings—for ever!

This situation looks rather frightening to the lover of bike racing at first, but it really could turn out to be a blessing in disguise. Where bike tracks *are* built, Liverpool and Canberra, for example, at least they will be in line with shapes and surfaces of the European arenas. No longer will Aussie riders have to go through the drama of becoming accustomed to European tracks . . . and vice versa. Many a World-rated European rider has been well and truly thrashed by even second raters in Australia in the years gone by. All this will be changed and international competition must become stronger for it.

Besides, the spectacle of throttle-control riding rather than the full-bore, fence-scraping tactics so necessary in Australia at present should develop a 'New breed' of Australian riders. Even the popularity of solo motorcycle speedway should improve once fans see it on tracks which emphasise the ability of the rider.

Action from the Australian Inter-State Solo Shield series with Bob Sharp leading Kevin Torpie at the Sydney Showground.

Who knows ... eventually such popularity could push the four-wheelers into the background and if sufficient tracks open for the two-wheelers, then a League competition on the East Coast of Australia would become a real proposition.

It could so easily happen, only time will tell.

DAVE BOOTH is editor of Australian *Speedway Action Pictorial*. Most of the photographs in this article were taken by *REVS Speedway World* staff photographer BILL MEYER.

13

THE UNLUCKIEST TEAM IN BRITAIN
That's Cradley United, claims Andrew Edwards

Cradley Heath, smack bang in the middle of the unromantic West Midlands industrial Black Country has been saddled with a tag they would very much like to lose—that of 'The Unluckiest Team in Britain'. But unfortunately they have earned it in the hardest possible way over many, many years and there are no other contenders to the title.

Cradley has always been something of an enigma in speedway. Today's big time glamour clubs have built up their success and reputations with superb on track performances, winning trophies galore and wowing the crowds with star riders and promoting prestige events.

The Midlanders however have never been in the big time, ever since speedway started at the track way back in 1947, when they were founder members of Division Three. What Cradley have had to face over the years would have forced most clubs out of existence. Just in recent years they have had to face the tragic death of one of the best up-and-coming young riders in the country, the loss of a Midlands stalwart through injury, the loss of an international rider through a tragic road accident and a long injury list which makes *Emergency Ward Ten* look like a story from *Noddy*.

The Cradley Supporters Club bar is devoid of any sparkling trophies. A dying club? No, just the opposite. Cradley continues to be the backbone of British speedway and has crowd attendances each week of the season, come rain or shine, that are the envy of speedway promoters the length and breadth of Britain.

The Cradley supporters, with their green, white and red rosettes and scarves, are known nationwide for their fanatical support of their team. They turn up in their thousands at the Dudley Wood track to cheer on their heroes. Not only is the

The late Ivor Hughes.

team volubly supported at home, the Cradley team is always followed by a large contingent of coaches and private cars on away trips.

Perhaps the answer lies in Cradley's poor record itself! One thing is for sure, Cradley speedway racing is never predictable or dull on the 367 yard track which most teams ride well. The team may lose by a point, win by a point or lose by ten, nobody can ever be sure. There are no boring runaway victories at Cradley.

In 1973 Cradley were particularly hard hit and went for weeks on end without scoring a victory at home because of one disastrous rider injury after another, but still the crowds kept pouring in in their thousands to cheer on the lads that were left.

Speedway supporters, like the riders they follow so avidly are bred tough, but Cradley supporters must be the toughest of the lot. They certainly have had to withstand more. In the British League, started only in 1965, Cradley have been wooden spoonists twice and their highest-ever position has been seventh.

Fate has dealt some awful blows to Cradley, none more so than that delivered in 1966. The night of August 20 will never be forgotten by Cradley fans. That night the young Welshman Ivor Hughes, just about to claim real fame with the Heathens, was killed in a triple crash. He was twenty-six.

Ivor's progress at Cradley that year was sensational. His British League debut was made at Dudley Wood against Newport in the last match of the 1965 season. He scored a third place in his first ride, a second to Johnny Hart and then fell twice. So the youngster, a plumber by trade from the Welsh village of Berriew, who once vowed 'I will ride my heart out for Cradley' moved on to greater promise in 1966. He became a contender for regular team places. At the very beginning of the campaign he showed flashes of his future form. At Coventry he scored five points from his three reserve rides.

Ivor bought himself a brand new Eso machine in June and he quickly blossomed into a man to be reckoned with. His great night soon came. Vargarna, the Swedish club side visited Cradley for a grand challenge match on August 6. Ivor top-scored for the Heathens with 10 points. The star attraction that night for the huge crowd was reigning World Champion Bjorn Knuttson, who went through the match unbeaten for 15 points.

Then he met Ivor in the scratch race final. It was one of the most memorable races ever seen during the long history of the club. Ivor beat the Swedish world champ fair and square—and nearly brought the house down. There was plenty

A Cradley Heath team photo from the early sixties—and in keeping with their unlucky reputation current team manager Harry Bastable nursing a broken arm at the time when he was one of the Heathens' top scorers. Other familiar faces include, third from left back row, Ivor Brown, John Hart (far right, back row) and kneeling on the far right is Stan Stevens, who was involved in the Lokeren mini-bus tragedy.

of celebrating in the bars afterwards and even today that race is recalled by reminiscing Cradley fans.

More was to come from Ivor. The following week he was the hero again when he top scored for Cradley against Swindon.

Then came the fateful night of August 20. Ivor had ridden magnificently to remain unbeaten against Sheffield. Then in the second half he was involved in a first bend crash with two Sheffield riders. He received serious head injuries and never regained consciousness. He died in a local hospital three days later. All Cradley mourned for Ivor, whose brilliant career turned out to be so tragically short.

He is remembered each year by the presentation of the Ivor Hughes Trophy to the outstanding Cradley junior of the year. At the time of his death he was acclaimed as the most improved rider in the country. During the months before the crash Ivor had risen from no more than an average rider into a star in the making. Around the Midlands he had already been tipped to reach the very top.

Ivor was the third Heathen to lose his life. Alan Hunt, who rode for many years for Cradley and England was killed in South Africa, although by then he had been transferred to Birmingham. Ray Beaumont was killed in a Cornwall grass track meeting. Ivor's was the first fatal crash at the Dudley Wood track.

Cradley hoped when the British League began they would have a change of luck. In the old Provincial League from 1960 Cradley always seemed to suffer any bad luck going around, especially with injuries to riders. But success unfortunately did not follow, only more heartaches.

The backbone of Cradley's Provincial League team was the King of the league, Ivor Brown, one of the most accomplished 'white line' riders of his era. Given an inch he would be through to the front. He was the one man who held Cradley together, especially when the team rode away from home. He was often criticised for his white line riding style, but his points return was essential to Cradley and he was the team's top scorer for many seasons. He was a maestro on tight tracks. Tiny Monmore Green, the home of Cradley's deadly rivals Wolverhampton was one of his favourite hunting grounds, indeed he held the track record there in 1963.

Ivor, 'Mr Cradley', was an important ingredient to any Cradley side with his long riding experience. He showed his liking of the new style league competition when he scored a maximum against Glasgow. His career was practically over two days later when he and five times world champion Ove Fundin tangled at the prestige Internationale at Wimbledon during the first race and on the first bend. Ivor was sent hurtling into the safety fence and received a hairline fracture of the spine, broken ribs and lacerations which sidelined him for most of the season.

It had been a fascinating year for Ivor, one of the leading Provincial League stars, pitting his wits against the more established aces from the old National League, and the Cradley rider had showed a lot of them they were not all the unbeatable supremos they had thought they were.

Ivor returned to racing too quickly. In only his third match against Coventry, he scored five points from his first three rides and then had to retire from the match. It was his last match of the season. He aggravated his back injury and had to have further treatment.

He returned to lead Cradley in 1966 and 1967 but it was never quite the same old Ivor. He was dogged by further injury. In 1968 he dislocated his shoulder at Belle Vue. Shortly after he had got over this he was sadly injured yet again and decided to retire.

In his shale career of 16 years he became one of the outstanding performers produced from Midland tracks. He has since become one of the sport's promoters, in the Second Division at Long Eaton.

The Cradley hoodoo can also outwit the speedway statisticians! In 1968 Cradley were tipped in a speedway paper to win the league—by statistics. By taking the calculated match average of each man in the team and adding them up Cradley it seemed came out on top. They finished 14th!

Injury problems were again the cause. Bob Andrews, the London-born, naturalised New Zealander was injured before he ever rode before his home fans. Wearing the CH jersey for the first time at an open meeting at Wolverhampton he had to lay his bike down to avoid a fallen rider and fractured his collar bone.

Then Cradley's first ever Swedish rider Tommy Bergqvist was injured no less than three times during the season. In the end the club were forced to sign another Swede as a replacement, Lars Jansson. Then he too was injured. Ivor Brown retired and two other Cradley riders also broke bones.

The Midland team was hit badly by the worst tragedy ever to strike at British speedway—the mini-bus crash at Lokeren, Belgium in 1970 which claimed the lives of four riders, West Ham's Martyn Piddock and Pete Bradshaw, Wimbledon's Garry Everett, Australian Malcolm Carmichael and the legendary King of Crash Phil Bishop. Cradley's captain Colin Pratt was seriously injured in the crash and he never rode again.

The party was returning home after a short trip to Holland, organised by Phil Bishop. Colin had won an individual event and helped a 'West Ham' side beat a Dutch team. Colin was one of England's leading riders at the time of the crash. He had shown terrific form only a couple of months before the crash when he twice defeated world champion Ivan Mauger in a league match at Cradley. He was told by a specialist that he should not ride again because bones in his neck had not set properly and another accident could leave him paralysed.

Colin had joined Cradley from Hackney at the beginning of the 1970 season and quickly established himself as a favourite with the Cradley crowds. Only weeks before the tragedy in Belgium Colin had accepted the captaincy of Cradley, after Roy Trigg had asked to be relieved of the post. Trigg introduced the late Malcolm Carmichael to the British scene and the Australian was a regular competitor in Cradley second half events.

The bad luck was taken so seriously it was decided to make a fresh start. Before the 1973 season Cradley decided on a wholesale new image in an attempt to get rid of, for once and for all, the bad luck bogey.

The new image consisted of new team colours, green, white AND red, and a new name Cradley 'United', instead of the Heathens and they also had a new team manager, ex-Cradley rider Harry Bastable. For a long time green has been thought of as an unlucky racing colour, but Cradley's idea of disguising the fact that they race in green, didn't work. They had so many injuries they filled a

Arthur Price

Howard Cole

Dave Perks

second Emergency Ward Ten—and once again finished bottom of the league.

Cradley grabbed just 18 points from their 34 league matches. Reading, who won the league, scored 51 points! And still the speedway-hungry crowds flocked through the Dudley Wood turnstiles each week.

Even with the new image Cradley didn't escape. Six out of the seven riders were injured at one time or another. Only local rider Dave Perks, the reserve came out of the campaign unscathed.

Sickening injuries began early. Howard Cole, one of the top English riders around, was to have been one of the team's kingpins. He made a remarkable comeback from terrible injuries received the season before in the British semi final round of the world championships at Leicester. He was allowed to make his comeback from the reserve berth by the Control Board, but was soon zipping in useful scores as though he had never been out of the game. Then came the crunch. After only six home matches Cole crashed heavily in the second half of the match with Hackney. To the dismay of the Cradley fans he was carried off—with a dislocated shoulder and a broken ankle. These injuries kept Howard out of action for three months of the season. In all he completed only 19 matches for Cradley, but finished as the club's top scorer.

That was only the beginning of a series of incidents in a season that all Cradley supporters would like to forget. Veteran Colin 'Joe' Gooddy crashed at Dudley Wood against Coventry and broke his collar bone, which put him out for a couple of months.

Bruce Cribb was the next victim. In an horrific crash, in which he cleared the safety fence and the width of the greyhound track, he received a double fracture of the leg which put him out for the season. Lars Hultberg, the young Swedish rider then broke a bone in his shoulder in Sweden and Cradley were having to rely heavily on guest riders.

Still the crowds poured in, mainly to see the most successful Heathen of all time, Swede Bernt Persson, the darling of the Cradley supporters and the first Cradley rider ever to reach a world final. But even the Cradley number one could not avoid the jinx in this season of seasons. He broke an arm in an incident with Anders Michanek in the Swedish national championships. And this year too the jinx has stuck. Young Dave Perks broke a leg, new signing Malcolm Corradine received facial injuries, returning Dave Younghusband gave up his comeback because of a back injury, and 1973 World Finalist John Boulger went out of the championship with a broken chain.

Once again Cradley were firmly pinned in the lower regions of the league—yet the crowds still poured into Dudley Wood.

Andrew Edwards is editor of *Motor Cycle News*' Speedway Slant column.

Cradley's league record:

National League Division Three	1947	2
	1948	2
National League Division Three	1949	4
	1950	3
	1951	15
	1952	4
Provincial League	1960	6
	1961	4
	1962	8
	1963	9
	1964	10
British League	1965	16
	1966	19
	1967	18
	1968	14
	1969	7
	1970	15
	1971	18
	1972	16
	1973	18

A broken leg while with the Heathens temporarily halted Bruce Cribb's scoring . . .

QUIZ ANSWERS

1   Cordy Milne, 1934.
2   Stamford Bridge. They won the Southern League in 1929.
3   J. A. Prestwich & Co. Ltd. of London N17.
4   Lonsdale Park Stadium, Workington.
5   Jack Chapman. He won the title in 1930.
6   Jack Parker.
7   Olle Nygren.
8   A team who rode in America in 1949.
9   Wimbledon beat Southampton 123-93 on aggregate.
10   1952. His first meeting was against Wembley on May 26 that year.
11   Ten in each league.
12   Trevor Redmond. He scored a 15 point maximum in the final at Cradley Heath in 1960.
13   Ken and Neil Middleditch; Reg and Eddie Reeves.
14   Barry Briggs.
15   Charlie Monk—on May 12th, 1965 at Poole.
16   Belle Vue.
17   They formed the British team that won the European Sand Track Team Championship in West Germany on Sunday October 22nd, 1967.
18   Ten teams—Belle Vue 2nd, Nelson, Middlesbrough, Plymouth, Rayleigh, Crayford, Canterbury, Reading, Weymouth and Berwick.
19   1968.
20   Zenon Plech.

14
ON PARADE IN '74
by Mike Patrick

Kings Lynn, 1974.

Weymouth 1974.

Five of the 1974 Boston side—left to right: Dave Piddock, David Gagen, Carl Glover, Russ Osborne and Robert Hollingworth.

Ignore those leathers—it's Newport's Reidar Eide.

England team manager Len Silver.

Swindon heat leader Norman Hunter.

Typical tigering from John Louis.

Canned again—America's Scott Autrey!

It looks like an old photograph—but in fact it's Phil Crump racing at Mildura, Victoria in his old Crewe race-jacket.

The superb style of 1971 World Champion Ole Olsen. Inset: Ole working on his machine.

15 | WIELKAPOLSKI TO GORZOW
by Ian MacDonald

Gorzow Wielkapolski is not the sort of place you would be likely to visit for a holiday . . . unless of course you happened to be a speedway fan. Then, you would be in excellent company, for Gorzow is a hot-bed of speedway interest. It is one of the speedway-mad areas of East Europe and compares with Ufa in Russia where, it seems, just everybody is a fan of speedway, zuzel or the black sport—call it what you will.

Gorzow, formerly Landsberg, is in the far west of Poland and is probably the nearest Polish town of significance to the East German border. When it comes to speedway you might say that Gorzow is the nearest town of significance to Great Britain! Life there revolves around the giant local engineering complex for six days of every week during the summer. On the seventh day, however, there is only one focal point and that is the Gorzow stadium—home of the local Stal speedway team.

Now, the Stal boys fancy themselves a bit. In the eyes of their fans they can do little wrong. Some even go as far as to say that Stal are fast approaching the position of being the world's number one club side. In the absence of a speedway equivalent to soccer's European Cup it is difficult to draw accurate comparisons between club sides from different nations. But were this possible the Stal side would be certainly amongst the leading two or three sides.

Yet just over a decade ago Stal were the great unknowns of Polish speedway. They were a struggling Second Division club eager to make progress but finding things rather difficult. Rybnik was the real centre of Polish speedway in those days and for Stal to imagine that they could build a team to take on and beat the Rybnik boys seemed very much a pipedream.

However, thanks to the co-operation of the Gorzow Engineering authorities who controlled the speedway team they were given every encouragement.

Stal were in dire need of a figurehead to lead the side and a rider to help train the many young boys who daily were applying for chances to become speedway riders. The Stal directors got the answer to both problems in the form of one rider. They played a masterstroke and signed Leszno's up-and-coming Andrzej Pogorzelski. At the time Pogorzelski was probably the best Polish rider not attached to the mighty Rybnik club and his move to Gorzow caused more than a few raised eyebrows.

However Pogorzelski seemed happy enough with the arrangement and it didn't take him long to prove that both club and rider had made the right decision. Stal improved out of all recognition. They ran away with the Second Division title and were promoted.

Straightaway they were a force in the First Division and were the team that Rybnik began to fear most. Pogorzelski headed the charts and together with Rybnik stars Antoni Woryna and Andrzej Wyglenda he gave the Polish national side a spearhead that was to take them to successive World Cup victories in 1966 and 1967.

Pogorzelski was the idol of Gorzow not only to the fans but also to the club's directors. Not only was he a prolific scorer, home and away, but as one Polish observer recounted to an English reporter, 'Ee is as you say in England, a barrel of laughs.'

A comedian or not, Pogorzelski took his racing with the utmost seriousness. And it was as a catalyst to the rest of the team that he probably made his most telling and long-lasting contribution.

In those early days his fellow Stal heat leaders were Edmund Migos and Jerzy Padewski. Two riders recognised as leading candidates for the international squad. But it was only when Pogorzelski got down to one of his training sessions with the youngsters that Migos and Padewski realised that they too had a lot more to offer in addition to scoring points.

Like Pogorzelski they worked tirelessly at the group training sessions and in the case of Migos, particularly, latent talents as a trainer were allowed to blossom. In fact Migos even surpassed Pogorzelski in this direction and became acknowledged as Poland's leading trainer.

Pogorzelski was also enthusiastic enough to boast that Stal, with a proper system of channeling youngsters into top grade racing, could become Poland's top club and make a serious claim to become a leading force in the world.

According to Pogorzelski there was absolutely no reason why Stal shouldn't reach a position of near invincibility in any ties conducted on an aggregate basis of home and away matches.

Such was the Gorzow dream. How near is it to bearing fruit? The answer is that they are well on their way. They have already enjoyed considerable success. They have wrested the league title away from Rybnik who unlike Stal did not dream of the future and have suffered with the passing of those early stars.

The second question must be: How much of Stal's recent success can be

Trainer Edmund Migos (left) with former World Finalist Henryk Glucklick.

Stal Gorzow's Edward Jancarz.

attributed to those Pogorzelski-Migos training sessions?

The answer here must be 'all of it'.

During the past six seasons Polish speedway has had three riders of real note. One is Jerzy Szczakiel from Opole and the other two are both pupils of the Gorzow stable. The Stal riders to benefit most from this specialised tuition are Edward Jancarz and Zenon Plech.

Jancarz, now 28, is ensuring that the Gorzow traditions continue. With both Pogorzelski, back at Leszno trying to work the oracle for his original and now ultra ambitious Leszno side, and Migos, sadly on the sidelines through a 1972 injury, missing from Gorzow it is Jancarz who is established as the top trainer.

In fact Jancarz carried on the excellent work started by his mentors in the training of the young Plech. Plech, too, is already putting something back into the sport and is helping Jancarz in the schooling of two of the newest Gorzow recruits.

Already their success in the field is beginning to show. The 1973 Young Poland side which toured Britain had Gorzow teenagers Ryszard Fabiszewski and Boguslaw Nowak in the line up. Both are the obvious successors to Plech but as he is still only in his early 20's it gives Gorzow the sort of potential heat leader trio for the middle 1970's which should put them well on their way to improving still further on that original Pogorzelski dream.

Remember, too, that Jancarz will still be playing a part so, in effect, Stal will have perhaps four of Poland's top half dozen riders on the books.

As well as team success the Stal fans have also been in no doubt that they would dearly love to boast a world champion of their own. Back in 1968 they looked to be well on the way to seeing this come true. Jancarz, then 22, had battled through to the World Final at Ullevi where, despite riding with three broken ribs, he finished third behind the mighty Kiwi duo of Mauger and Briggs.

The Stal fans eagerly awaited the immediate seasons when they felt sure that Jancarz would surely improve upon this. The main target was the 1970 World Final. For almost twelve months prior to this Polish-staged classic there was talk of the impending Mauger-Jancarz clash. Neither rider had even ridden in one 1970 qualifying round but the Gorzow folk were already in no doubt. 'It will be a two horse race,' they said, 'One will be first, the other second, and the rest nowhere.' In part they were correct in the prediction. One of them did win but that was Mauger. Poor old Jancarz never even made it to the final. He was ruled out of the qualifying rounds with collarbone problems!

The mighty clash of the century didn't happen.

It has been a tough road back for Jancarz but he has made it. In the meantime Plech has blossomed into the real glamour star of Gorzow and Poland. It is a position that the modest and level-headed Jancarz is happy to concede. Carrying on in the best Gorzow traditions he invariably spends as much time helping Plech during a meeting as he does in looking after his own interests.

Perhaps he, like Pogorzelski and Migos, doesn't have that spark or almost fanatical will to win and this is where Plech is so much of a new departure for the Stal side. He likes to win at all times. He hates to lose but still manages to keep his feelings to himself. He has picked up a great deal from his various trainers but he has a mind and ideas of his own. He weighs the one against the other and decides just how far he dare deviate from the path he has been taught. Influenced by others? Certainly. An out-and-out copycat? Definitely no!

Plech wants to learn from everybody. He has been lucky. He had an enviable early grounding. He has a constant advisor in the form of Jancarz and he was, thanks to the 1974 World Superstars series, able to watch at the closest of quarters, masters like Mauger, Briggs, Moore, Fundin and Olsen.

So Plech remains Poland's best hope for world success in the next five years or so. In Nowak and Fabiszewski as European Finalists this year they have two riders ready to take over if Plech falters somewhere along the line. Just in case any of them get a little too cocky about it all there are plenty of other whizz kids in the Gorzow pipeline only too keen to grab their chance. Gorzow have been nursing their dreams since the early 1960's. Already they have made their mark. The time to go for the jackpot can't be all that far away.

One of the greatest teachers of all—double world champion Ronnie Moore who made a fleeting comeback in 1974 as a guest for Coventry while in Britain for the World Team Cup qualifying round.

16

NURSING AMBITIONS OF GREATNESS
by Dave Stevens

Speedway riders are not made. Unlimited cash to buy the best equipment and tuition is not sufficient to become a world star. Indeed, the opposite is often the case, for speedway is full of riders who started with nothing and by sheer hard work and dedication reached the top.

None more so than Ivan Mauger.

In plain, simple terms he was a flop when he first arrived at Wimbledon, heralded the new 'White Hope' of New Zealand speedway. Ivan made no impression with the Dons, and fared little better in the amateur Southern Area League circles. But he never lost his dedication. He returned home, licked his wounds, and set about proving himself the best in the sport. Initially, it was on the New Zealand tracks.

When he could learn no more he moved on to Australia and eventually returned to England to join Newcastle. What was promised before became a reality. He was a match for the best, and very soon became *the* best.

Nowadays, Ivan imparts the knowledge that has made him a superstar to youngsters whose one ambition is to topple him from the top perch.

Ivan is not alone. Fellow New Zealander Barry Briggs who, like Ivan was chasing a fifth World Championship crown this year, always has a word for the struggling novice, and those on the first rung of the ladder.

Like Wimbledon junior Pete Wigley. He is on loan to Rye House to gain regular league racing experience in Division Two circles, but was as overjoyed as the Dons senior executives when Bee-Bee finally confirmed his agreement to return to British League racing at Plough Lane.

'Just being around and watching Barry is an education,' says Pete. 'I will learn a lot from that alone.'

Division One still produces the occasional overnight sensation, but it is to their Division Two brothers where most of them turn when replacements are needed each winter.

H

Many senior tracks have a nursery of their own in Division Two. Hackney have Rye House (now a pukka league circuit for the first time, incidentally, but long a recognised training track for the sport); Ipswich look to Birmingham; King's Lynn around the Wash to Boston; Leicester have links with Teesside; Oxford with Eastbourne. Others, like Belle Vue and Poole have their own development programme.

Belle Vue have regular winter training sessions at their Hyde Road track, hopeful of unearthing one or two potential new team members each year. Poole have their own training track, in the New Forest at Matchams Park, Ringwood.

In addition to training sessions, practice meetings are often held and for the day's best riders there is the opportunity of a 'proving' second-half ride at Poole.

Tracks not so fortunate with nursery or training facilities still encourage juniors. At times it needs little more of the 'hopeful' than to knock on the promoter's office door and ask for a second-half ride. Few promoters will pass up the chance of passing by another Ivan Mauger! But once out on the track the novice has to prove himself, and double quick. Not necessarily by winning races, or going fast. Potential is what is looked for and if the novice shows that he will quickly be offered a contract, trained through the track's development programme and when ready, usually loaned out to a lower section side to gain team racing experience.

Division Two is fortunate in having several 'old hands' who act as rider/coaches. Reg Trott, who for years partnered legendary Swedish star Ove Fundin at Norwich, played a major role in developing Eastbourne trainees to British League standards when the Eagles entered Division Two in 1969.

Former World Finalists Mike Broadbanks and Ken McKinlay are currently doing likewise for Stoke and Scunthorpe, and the sport generally.

'I must admit that moving down into Division Two was a blow to my pride,' says Broadbanks of his switch to Stoke in 1973 after nearly 20 years in top circles.

'But after only a couple of meetings I found myself enjoying speedway again.'

'Broadie' enjoyed his racing not so much for the points money—'Although that's always useful,' he admits—but because of the attitudes of his rivals.

'I never had the impression that the kids felt I was taking *their* prize money. They seemed pleased to be able to race against me, and doubly pleased when they won.

'And I didn't mind that, either. In a good many instances I'd already told 'em how to do it. Following their back wheel and watching them put advice into practice was very rewarding.'

Most junior opportunities are created in the winter months, when training facilities abound, but there are year-long activities too, like at Hackney and on a former Ack-Ack gun site at Iwade in Kent. There, Hackney's England international Barry Thomas has carved a track out of the ground almost virtually by hand. He admits that the training facilities offered are a business, part of his overall speedway earnings, but if he only invested the money and time consumed on some other project he would produce better returns.

So too would most of the others. But to a man they all recognise the help they had when they first started speedway. They appreciate that unless there is someone around to guide the newcomers today then in a few short years they will not have the opposition around to keep them on their toes.

Passing on advice at Wimbledon—Barry Briggs.

17

DIVISION TWO GALLERY

Roger Wright (Teesside)

Graham Jones (Berwick)

Malcolm Mackay (Workington)

Paul O'Neil (Barrow)

Mike Lanham (Peterborough)   *Bobby McNeil (Eastbourne)*

Trevor Barnwell, Allen Emmett (both Rye House) and Crewe's Les Ott deep in thought.

Phil Herne (Birmingham)   *Terry Barclay (Canterbury)*

18 THE WINGED WHEEL OF SUCCESS~
A Retrospective Look at the World Championship Over the Years by Peter Oakes

Those of you with long memories or an encyclopaedic knowledge of speedway will know that long before the World Championship became an official fixture there were several bids to stage what were claimed to be Championships of the World. But nowhere in the record books will you find any evidence other than the date 1936 as the beginning of the World Championship as we know today.

By then speedway had grown out of its birth pangs and had developed into a sport enjoyed and watched by millions. And the 1936 World Championship was truly the first time that riders from all over the world were allowed to compete. Entries were invited (and as far as records go there was no stipulating qualifying mark to be reached by would-be World Champions) and a total of 63 riders were given official recognition and took part in a series of qualifying rounds.

Today—on Second Division tracks alone—a total of 90 riders are competing in the preliminary rounds with another 70 coming in at the Division One qualifying rounds stage . . . and that is in Britain alone!

But to go back to 1936 the original 63 represented 12 nations—England, Australia, America, South Africa, France, Rumania, Sweden, Spain, Germany, Canada and New Zealand—and at the end of the day, after a complicated system of scoring under which Australian Bluey Wilkinson scored an unbeaten 15 point maximum on final night but finished no higher than third in the competition, it was another Australian Lionel Van Praag who became the first-ever World Speedway Champion.

Then, as now, it was THE glamour event with £500 as the first prize—an enormous sum in 1936.

Learning from initial mistakes there was a slight revision of the rules for the second year of the competition, but the heavily criticised bonus points system (each rider had gone into the final with an average score from his qualifying

The first three in the 1973 World Final—Ivan Mauger (runner-up) champion Jerzy Szczakiel and third place man Zenon Plech.

rounds) remained. Fortunately this time the man who won on the night also won on the season—and America celebrated with its first-ever World Champion: Jack Milne, now a thriving Californian businessman closely connected with the revival of speedway in the States in recent years.

A massive 85,000 crowd paid then record receipts at Wembley to see a Yankee whitewash with Milne's compatriots Wilbur Lamoreaux and Cordy Milne filling the minor placings on the victory dais.

By now the rumblings of discontent in Germany were heard and 1938 was to be the last season the World Final was actually staged in pre-war Britain. It was also the year that, for the first time, riders from the Second Division were allowed to compete in the title chase.

An even bigger crowd than the previous year—this time 90,000—reflected the sport's true status and once again it was the much-maligned bonus points system that produced a winner . . . Australian Bluey Wilkinson.

He and defending champion Jack Milne each scored 14 points on the night (Wilkinson dropped his point to Milne; and Milne dropped his to fellow country-man Lamoreaux) but rather than a sudden death run-off the title was decided by the number of points scored in the previous qualifying round! In this instance Wilkinson started off with eight points on final night and Milne seven.

The storm clouds were gathering but everyone thought that Hitler would delay his invasion until after the 1939 World Final (not necessarily suggesting that he was a speedway fan!) and everything built up to another grand occasion with previous winners Milne and Van Praag prominent among the qualifiers for the championship.

In fact four days before the meeting was due to be staged at Wembley war was declared and the World Speedway Final became an early victim of the German campaign.

Could Milne have won his second World title? Would Van Praag have completed his personal double? Or would a new name have gone on the scroll of honour? It's a question no-one could answer then let alone now but there are many who claim that Milne would have regained his crown and he was, indeed, leading bonus point scorer among the final qualifiers.

There was to be a ten year break before the next World Championship was held although in 1946, 1947 and 1948 an individual competition was staged and has since been recognised as a World Final.

Because of the contingencies of war many foreigners were unable to compete and consequently the 1946 competition was labelled the British Riders' Championship; the 1947 event was the Speedway Riders' Championship; and in 1948 the

Americans reappeared in the Riders' Championship and the sport attracted a Royal guest of honour—the Duke of Edinburgh—to present the trophy and awards to Australian Vic Duggan.

By 1949 it was decided that the World Championship should be revived and with a total of 224 competitors—including many from the Continent—the competition was staged along the lines that we recognise so readily today.

Tommy Price—the man who had won the British Riders' Championship in '46—proved that he was the best in the world with a 15-point maximum in front of 93,000 fans who cheered an English clean sweep of the top four places . . . the first and only time since the War that any nation has provided each of the top four scorers. With each passing season so somebody—somewhere—set up some sort of World Championship record.

In 1950 that great Australian Jack Young became the first Second Division rider to reach the World Final—he actually finished top of the qualifying scorers after fighting his way through the preliminary rounds—but saw Freddie Williams take the title back to Wales. A season later Young became the first Second Division rider to win the title—after the late Jackie Biggs had fallen in his final ride needing only one point to take the championship!

More history in 1952, when British riders actually took part in qualifying rounds on the Continent and Youngie became the first man to win the crown in two successive seasons. The now veteran, then youthful, Olle Nygren became the second Swedish rider to reach the last sixteen (Dan Forsberg had qualified twelve months earlier) and Rune Sormander, set a new high standard by qualifying even though he didn't ride regularly in Britain. With Welshman Williams regaining his crown he prevented another slice of history: a possible third-in-a-row victory for Young.

It was Williams again who provided the sensation of 1954—by failing to qualify for a place in the last 16 . . . the first time the defending champion had not been on hand to do just that save for injury or retirement. New Zealand provided her first World Champion: Ronnie Moore and Wembley debutants included Barry Briggs, Peter Craven and Ove Fundin.

Craven, later to meet such an untimely racing death in Scotland, became England's second World Champion in 1955 when the four leading scorers from the Continent were seeded direct to Wembley; and a year later Peter became the first recipient of a new rule that saw the reigning World Champion automatically on hand to defend his championship by direct seeding to the final itself.

A year later it was Sweden's turn to celebrate . . . when Ove Fundin won the first of his five titles and over the next decade it was Fundin, Craven, Moore and the 1957 title-winner Barry Briggs who dominated proceedings.

Highlights of some of those years saw Josef Hofmeister become Germany's first final qualifier in 1957; the Sunday Pictorial (the title later changed to the Sunday Mirror) take over sponsorship of the championship in 1958 when the now familiar winger-wheel award was designed; in 1959 Mike Polukard became Poland's first World Finalist; in 1960 three Poles reached the last sixteen; and in '61 the great Fundin became the first man to win three World Finals.

By then a new Swedish name had cropped up—Bjorn Knutsson, and even though he had to wait until 1965 to break the Moore-Fundin-Briggs-Craven stranglehold he was runner-up twice; fourth once; and fifth before winning a deserved title in 1965.

In 1961 Igor Plechanov became Russia's first World Finalist and in 1964 became the first Iron Curtain rider to finish on the rostrum although a year earlier Boris Samorodov—later to become a World Ice-Speedway Champion—was only a point adrift of third place.

Twice Plechanov finished as runner-up and in 1966 Sverre Harrfedlt became the first Norwegian to share World honours when he, too, was runner-up.

Fundin, meanwhile, had won his fourth crown (naturally the first man to do it) and anxious to keep one jump ahead of Briggs (who won his fourth title in 1966) he made it five wins in 1967—the season a new name appeared at the forefront of the World Championship: Ivan Mauger.

He had finished fourth on his final debut in 1966 and third a year later. In 1968, in 1969, and in 1971 he took the top place to become the first rider to win three titles in three years; and the first man to win in three different countries.

When you realise one of these title successes came in the first final to be held outside Europe (behind the Iron Curtain in Poland) you have a measure of that achievement.

By now the championship was truly global and in 1971 Mauger had to be content with a runner-up berth behind Denmark's first motor-sport World Champion Ole Olsen.

John Louis became the first British League Division Two product to reach a World Final in 1972 when the legendary Barry Briggs finished what everyone thought was his farewell final appearance on a stretcher after a nasty crash put him out of the running at a time when he looked capable of taking his fifth world title.

Instead Mauger took his fourth in five years.

And so to 1973 and yet again the history books had a new entry: the first World Champion from Poland . . . Jerzy Szczakiel.

Again Szczakiel made history this year by failing to qualify for a final night championship defence, falling in his first ride as reigning title-holder!

ROLL OF HONOUR

1936	Lionel Van Praag (Australia & Wembley)
1937	Jack Milne (America & New Cross)
1938	Bluey Wilkinson (Australia & West Ham)
*1946	Tommy Price (England & Wembley)
*1947	Jack Parker (England & Belle Vue)
*1948	Vic Duggan (Australia & Harringay)
1949	Tommy Price (England & Wembley)
1950	Freddie Williams (Wales & Wembley)
1951	Jack Young (Australia & Edinburgh)
1952	Jack Young (Australia & West Ham)
1953	Freddie Williams (Wales & Wembley)
1954	Ronnie Moore (New Zealand & Wimbledon)
1955	Peter Craven (England & Belle Vue)
1956	Ove Fundin (Sweden & Norwich)
1957	Barry Briggs (New Zealand & Wimbledon)
1958	Barry Briggs (New Zealand & Wimbledon)
1959	Ronnie Moore (New Zealand & Wimbledon)
1960	Ove Fundin (Sweden & Norwich)
1961	Ove Fundin (Sweden & Norwich)
1962	Peter Craven (England & Belle Vue)
1963	Ove Fundin (Sweden & Norwich)
1964	Barry Briggs (New Zealand & Swindon)
1965	Bjorn Knutsson (Sweden)
1966	Barry Briggs (New Zealand & Swindon)
1967	Ove Fundin (Sweden & Belle Vue)
1968	Ivan Mauger (New Zealand & Newcastle)
1969	Ivan Mauger (New Zealand & Belle Vue)
1970	Ivan Mauger (New Zealand & Belle Vue)
1971	Ole Olsen (Denmark & Wolverhampton)
1972	Ivan Mauger (New Zealand & Belle Vue)
1973	Jerzy Szczakiel (Poland)
1974	

*Not official World Finals—see story.

19 | STEVE REINKE A PROFILE OF AN AUSTRALIAN SUPERSTAR

The term 'superstar' is used a little loosely these days but there can be little doubt that in 25-year-old Ipswich sensation Steve Reinke Australia has found yet another rider ready to take on the very best in the world . . . and beat them.

Reinke, the first Queenslander to win his country's national title in the space of no less than 41 years since Vic Huxley captured the event back in 1933. In post-Second World war years it has been dominated by New South Welshmen—Vic Duggan (1945, 1947, 1948), Frank Dolan (1946), Keith Ryan (1952), Aub Lawson (1949, 1950, 1953, 1954, 1955), Bob Sharp (1960, 1965) and Jim Airey (1967, 1968, 1969 and 1971).

Between them have been Jack Parker, Ulf Eriksson, Mike Broadbanks, Ken McKinlay, Chum Taylor and John Boulger, who has won the crown twice.

And now Reinke. Reinke, the first rider ever to capture the title without the benefit of extensive overseas experience.

When he won the title New Zealand was the only other country he had raced in, yet the experts are always claiming that in today's modern speedway world no rider could possibly hit the top without at least two seasons in British League racing.

Reinke has proved them wrong. Reinke, the top performer on either side in the 1973-1974 Australia v Great Britain test series. Reinke, the winner of the Australian Wills Internationale against a galaxy of seasoned stars in his first major meeting at the Sydney Royale, rated a tough track for quarter mile riders to master. Reinke, the backmarker, holder of the three-lap track record and winner of the Radio 41P Inter-Nations Cup this past season on his home bowl, the Brisbane Exhibition track.

What a fabulous season for a rider perhaps never previously mentioned in quite the same breath as Jimmy Airey, John Boulger or even John Langfield.

Reinke not only had not had the benefit of European experience . . . he was reluctant to go jetting off to join the professionals.

Even though he was offered at least three contracts—one by British Lions

Speeding around Brisbane's Exhibition Ground, 1974 Australian Champion Steve Reinke, a late season signing by Exeter.

manager Reg Fearman who wanted the Ipswich youngster to join the long list of Kangaroos he has used at Halifax over the years; one by new Division One track Hull; and a third by West Country big spenders Exeter—Reinke turned them all down, for a time preferring to stay at home running his motor-cycle business.

Fearman was most impressed by the Queenslander but even he couldn't persuade Reinke to forsake his native Ipswich for the colder climes of Halifax on a wet Spring evening! And until Exeter tempted him in July he stayed at home.

Steve, of course, is in a different position to that of the many young hopefuls who normally join the jet-setters each year. He owns a successful motor-cycle business, is right on top racing-wise and is married—to the daughter of Australian Speedway Control Board secretary Noel Stitt, a relationship which caused opponents to point the finger on a few occasions after race incidents in the years when Mr. Stitt served as the Australian Speedway Control Board's steward.

Steve was an overnight sensation when he entered speedway racing five years ago. He came from the short circuit ranks where he had won the Australian Senior 500 c.c. title at the Tivoli Circuit, near Ipswich.

When he started beating the likes of Bert Kingston, Jack and Doug White (not related by the way), Bryan Loakes, Peter Ingram, Les Bentzen and Kev Torpie everyone started to take an interest in the clean-cut good-looking Queenslander.

He was 'star' material in all ways. Then, just when he'd hit the top, he suffered head injuries in a heavy spill on the fast Ipswich half-kilometre granite-surfaced oval.

The next few times we saw Steve he was in a slump, finishing third or fourth in scratch races with the odd second thrown in. But Kingo and Whitey were all-dominant and even Reinke's style had appeared to fall off a little.

Often a rider in speedway has that one big season on top before he slides back to a position where he might stay for years, perhaps the rest of his career.

An injury . . . inability to outlay money for the best equipment . . . family responsibilities . . . a lack of dedication. There can be a dozen reasons involved. Reinke, though, like that well-advertised brand of hair cream, came back. During the 1971-1972 season he chased the handicap pointscore on a hard, reliable basis. In the end he missed the prize, won by Bobby Gourlay, but he'd proved that he could again come from behind White and company to collect the plaudits.

He provided a major shock when, in his first meeting outside Queensland, he went to Adelaide for the national title.

Steve Reinke, immediately before the 1974 Australian Championship.

Rated a real outsider, the tearaway who wouldn't be able to handle the pole-hugging fast line around Rowley Park, Reinke tied with local Johnny Boulger on points for third spot but was beaten in a run-off. The title, not unexpectedly went to Sydney's Airey.

In the 1972-1973 season Reinke again chased that elusive Brisbane handicap pointscore but again missed narrowly. He badly injured his right hand in a fall towards the end of the season. But before that he'd turned in some unbelievable rides.

It was a common sight to see front-markers two or three abreast with then up-and-comer Johnny Titman going round them, Jack White out further bouncing off the boards also trying to pass—and Steve Reinke, front wheel up the fence with everything wrapped on in turn trying to pass the whole lot!

At one stage we thought that they'd have to take the furniture out of the speedway office to create a racing chute for White and Reinke: they'd have ridden ten wide if they'd had to!

The result was the most hair-raising and exciting solo racing seen on the East Coast in donkey's years and the fans lapped it up.

They came to grief a few times, but their company out on the track was good, experienced and not lacking in know-how in a tight situation.

So onto the 1973-1974 season and the question: what would racing have in store for Steve Reinke? The boy had what it takes, could he now put it all together? Could he ever!

Again he was his hard charging self in the furious Brisbane handicaps—most of it televised in several Australian States as a regular Saturday morning feature—while a probable slight improvement in his gating saw him dominant all season in the scratch events.

A week before winning the Inter-Nations Cup against a star-studded Brisbane line-up, he had tracked down to Sydney for the Wills Internationale—in which he'd met Ole Olsen, Peter Collins, Reg Wilson, Jimmy McMillan, Antoni Woryna and the local hero, Billy-the-kid Sanders.

Sydney's massive Showground track has never been a happy hunting ground for banana-country men in general. Could Reinke rattle the Harbour City rockets? He gated superbly, fell into the quick, fence-scraping groove immediately, and showed fierce competitive determination.

It looked a clash between Peter Collins and the young Sanders after Billy had beaten Steve narrowly in their second outing—after feeding the visitor a wheel in a torrid first corner.

Then Reinke out-trapped the stylish Englishman to win and leave Sanders as the only undefeated rider. But then, in turn, Collins downed the Sydney youngster.

Three riders—Reinke, Collins and Sanders—on 14 points and needing a run-off to decide the issue.

This, unfortunately, turned out to be an anti-climax. Collins, moving back into position, was left as the tapes flew up. Reinke, making no mistakes, was gone.

Collins rounded-up Sanders, who blew a front tyre, and gave chase but Reinke was streaking out in front . . . and so became the first Queenslander to win a major solo trophy on the Sydney Royale. A great effort and the crowd rose to him.

In the 1973-1974 test series he was the only rider not to fall below double figures in any match—on either side!

British stars Peter Collins and Reg Wilson almost matched him—but each had one so-called 'failure'.

Steve topped the match averages for both teams in four appearances . . . and only two of those were on his home track at Brisbane. He should have made it five test appearances but Cyclone Wanda—it devastated much of Brisbane and the surrounding countryside bringing with it the worst floods of the century— blew him out and prevented him from flying down to Sydney for the final test.

He captained Australia for the first time in one test—the sixth—and led the Kangaroos to their only win of the series after going through his three second half rides undefeated.

So he had everything going for him when the 1974 Australian Championship rolled around in March—on the Brisbane track.

But still there was John Boulger—defending champ, Australia's number one, and fit again—plus Titman, White, Phil Crump and Langfield. All were genuine threats.

Methodically Boulger and Reinke disposed of them all—not too easily in some cases though—until they both stood unbeaten with their last ride to come.

And they were set against each other in heat 18—the crunch and almost certainly the title decider.

Steve drew the inside with Boulger out in three and they rocketed into the first turn shoulder to shoulder with Steve fighting to get up into the outside dirt first.

He made it . . . by a whisker.

Reinke led the way with Boulger throwing out everything, but there was no chance of Steve throwing it away now. A fabulous maximum in front of his home crowd. The old Ecka went mad acclaiming its hero.

Capping his season, Steve then raced in New Zealand with fellow Aussies John Boulger, Jim Airey and John Titman, forming the nucleus of a Rest of the World side which went down 55-53 to the touring British Lions at Auckland.

The Aussie foursome contributed 42 of the team's points—with Reinke, on his first-ever appearance outside Australia, rattling up seven.

Reinke, flanked by British Lions tourists Jim McMillan (left) and Reg Wilson

STEVE REINKE'S 1973-1974 RACING RECORD

TEST MATCHES:

AUSTRALIA:

Third Test match v British Lions (Adelaide)	12 points
Fourth Test match v British Lions (Sydney)	13 points
Fifth Test match v British Lions (Brisbane)	11 points
Sixth Test match v British Lions (Brisbane)	15 points

REST OF THE WORLD:

First Test match v British Lions (Auckland)	7 points

AUSTRALIAN INTER STATE SOLO SHIELD

QUEENSLAND:

v Western Australia	4 rides	12 points
v South Australia	4 rides	8 points
v Victoria	4 rides	11 points
v New South Wales	4 rides	12 points
at Western Australia	4 rides	7 points
at South Australia		rained off
at Victoria	4 rides	8 points
at New South Wales	4 rides	10 points

Overall average: 10.8.

This article is reprinted courtesy of Australia's leading motor-cycle magazine *REVS Motor Cycle News*. The author was DAVE BOOTH and photographs by Bill Meyer.

SHUTTER~SPEED
by Mike Patrick

Ace photographer MIKE PATRICK picks out six of his best Speedway photos —and tells you why.

Dust and television lights provide the background to this spectacular shot of Sweden's Christer Lofqvist taken with a Pentax, 135 mm lens, 250th @ F 2.8.

The split second that Anders Michanek broke the tapes in the 1973 World Final shot with a Nikon 135 mm lens, 250th of a second @ F 5.6.

When I was a youngster my bedroom walls were covered with glossy photos of all my favourite riders and many pleasurable hours were spent looking through the heavy pages of my carefully prepared Woolworths scrapbooks. If anyone had told me then that in years to come, I would be the man behind the camera posing up the idols that I worshipped at that time, I would have hit them with my lollipop.

The life of a photo-journalist in speedway is not as glamorous as may appear on the surface. For nine months of the year it's a solid slog spending most of each day couped up in a clammy darkroom completely unaware of what's happening in the outside world. But despite all that, I love the sport and the many friends that I have made since coming into the business.

When Ivan first asked me to choose the five favourite speedway shots that I had taken, the thought of ploughing through 30,000 negatives brought me out into a hot sweat. I needn't have worried. Sixty seconds later my choice had been made. I have individual reasons for choosing each photo, but there are two factors common to all, these are composition and split-second timing. If there was a way that I could cover every square inch of the track from every conceivable angle at the same time, my work would be easy. The composition of these five photographs could have been completely different if I had been standing just a couple of feet

One of the best action photographs of all time as Wimbledon's Neil Cameron climbs onto Barry Crowson (Kings Lynn). Camera: Nikon F 105 mm lens, 500th @ F 4.

Taking a dive . . . Poland's Zenon Plech with Australia's John Titman preparing for the worst. Technical data: Nikon F 135 mm lens, 250th at F 8.

from where I was positioned or if I had not fired the shutter at that precise moment. I'll use the Zenon Plech picture as an example. I have seen another photograph of this incident taken at exactly the same time and no more than six feet to my right. The other photo, although still good, lacked impact and looked a little messy. Plech was more side on and only half of Titman's bike and body were in the picture.

Crashes in speedway are inevitable and if they are going to happen anyway, I would be lying if I said that I didn't want to be in the right place at the right time. I know for a fact that if a crash is spectacular and results in nothing more than a few bruises and a sore bottie, then there is nothing that the boys concerned like more than to look through the photos and see how it all happened and perhaps learn where they went wrong.

Some tracks give better and more spectacular photos than others, Sheffield, Leicester and Wimbledon being top of the list but every track has a patch of its own where the riders look better than at any other part of the circuit and that's where I keep my sights aimed. For the amateur photographers here is a list of the equipment that I use:

Nikon F cameras, Nikon F2 motordrive, Nikon lenses 50mm, 85mm, 105mm, 135mm, 200mm, Novoflex 280mm. Pentacon 6 camera with 80mm and 180mm lenses and a Rollei T. All film, paper and materials are by Kodak.

This is what speedway's all about. Peter Collins leads Russia's Grigory Chlynovski (outside) and Sweden's Tommy Jansson. Nikon F 135 mm lens, 250th at F 8.

The back of the book . . .